THE BEST
PIANO
BUYER'S
GUIDE

KIM RAWLINGS

About the Author

Kim Rawlings has been tuning, repairing, rebuilding, refinishing, and selling pianos for more than twenty-five years. He started his career in the early 1970s at one of the West's largest piano retailers. Kim was involved in all aspects of the technical servicing and sales of pianos. He started his own piano retail store in 1980 and soon developed three additional piano retail outlets. Kim is presently the Head Piano Technician for one of the largest piano retailers in America. He has also maintained his own piano servicing business.

Kim's piano servicing abilities have made it possible for him to tune for many great pianists and musicians. From the early 1970s until the present, he has tuned for many artists when they performed in his area. The list includes George Shearing, Liberace, Lawrence Welk, Elton John, Count Basie, David Lanz, Wladimir Jan Kochanski, Suzanne Ciani, Tanya Tucker, the Osmonds, Harry Belafonte, Johnny Mathis, Jim Brickman, Lorie Line, Bob Hope, Barry Manilow, Melissa Manchester, Oscar Peterson, and others.

His unique perspective has enabled him to write this "MUST" book for anyone interested in purchasing any piano. This book is easy to understand and provides the consumer with enough knowledge to make a wise buying decision.

ACKNOWLEDGEMENTS

A special thanks to the manufacturers who so willingly provided me with the specifications on their pianos. I thank them for their cooperation and for their beautiful instruments that add so much of value to our society.

David Lanz, one of America's best "New Age" pianists, portrays in his composition "Cristofori's Dream" the story of the seventeenth-century Italian inventor Bartolomeo di Francesco Cristofori, who, building on the work of many predecessors, invented the modern piano. I particularly thank those piano manufacturers who keep trying to improve this magnificent invention with its capacity to give us music and bring us joy.

As the father of eight, I can think of few skills as valuable as musical training in a family. The piano has helped our children concentrate and focus, experience strong emotions, and thrill with achievement. Their musical ability has strengthened their scholastic performance and even improved their athletic ability.

A piano could easily be the greatest investment I ever made for a better quality of life for me and my children. So go on, buy a good piano!

1
Introduction

The children want to play the piano. The family has met. So the decision has been made. How do you find just the right instrument for your home? The search can be pleasant and exciting-- with no buyer's remorse--when you know what makes an excellent piano.

Most piano salesmen are honest people doing their best, but they have a tough job. Salesmen are almost always on commission and need to sell you a piano to pay their bills. After visiting a few dealers for information about their product, you could become so confused it would be easy to decide that the children should play violin or guitar--anything but the piano. Resist this temptation! A piano is the best instrument for a musical foundation.

Listen to all the information a sales representative gives you. Armed with the knowledge you gain from this book, ask knowledgeable questions and make careful hands-on evaluations. Then make an informed decision about which piano to purchase.

Here are three factors you need to consider before the search begins.

WHO IS THE PIANO FOR?

If the primary user is a beginner, the piano you choose may be very different from the one you choose if the primary user is very accomplished. I think many children quit playing the piano because their parents did not purchase an adequate piano for them. Resist the temptation to buy a piano just because the price is low. If your child learns to play well, then the extra money paid to purchase a good instrument will be a great investment. If your child quits because of an inadequate instrument, then the investment will be a bad one no matter how low the price.

HOW MUCH ROOM DO YOU NEED?

A short vertical and tall vertical piano take up the same floor area if they both have 88 notes (a standard keyboard). With bench, a vertical piano will need a width of about 5 feet, and a depth of 4½ to 5 feet.

A grand piano will need a width of about 5 feet; the depth will vary according to the model. Remember to add a couple of feet for the bench to the overall length. If a grand is 5 feet 7 inches long, you will need 7½ feet of depth to accommodate it.

It is important to position the piano where there will be no echos and where the sound will be evenly distributed throughout the room.

MONEY!

Usually, a used upright in playable condition will cost between $400 and $1,000. More recently built used verticals will cost $1,000 to $2,500. A used grand in playable condition will cost $3,500 to $5,500.

An adequate new vertical piano will cost about $3,500, and an adequate new grand will cost about $7,500. I do not recommend spinet pianos. (See pp. 14 and 18.) As a general rule, a studio-sized piano is the best value, combining lowest cost with highest quality.

You should also budget about $150 a year for maintenance. A piano needs to be tuned a couple of times per year. It will also periodically need regulation and repairs. Proper maintenance is crucial so that you can gain maximum value from your piano.

HOW A PIANO WORKS
THE SKELETON OF A VERTICAL PIANO (Drawing 1)

The back (1) of a vertical piano is the wooden frame to which the pinblock (2) is attached, the cast-iron plate (3) is bolted, and the soundboard (4) is glued.

It is important that the back posts (5) are well seasoned so that they won't warp. The back and posts help to support about 20 tons of tension. The most common woods used for back posts are poplar, beech, maple, oak, mahogany, and spruce. The action (10) consists of movable parts that cause a felt hammer to strike the string (7) which is attached to the tuning pin (6). The tuning pin goes through the plate and into the pinblock. The strings are strung on the plate and cross over the bass and treble bridges (8), thus transmitting the sound to the soundboard for amplification. The pedals (11) add expression and sustain notes during performances.

DRAWING 1
SKELETON OF VERTICAL PIANO

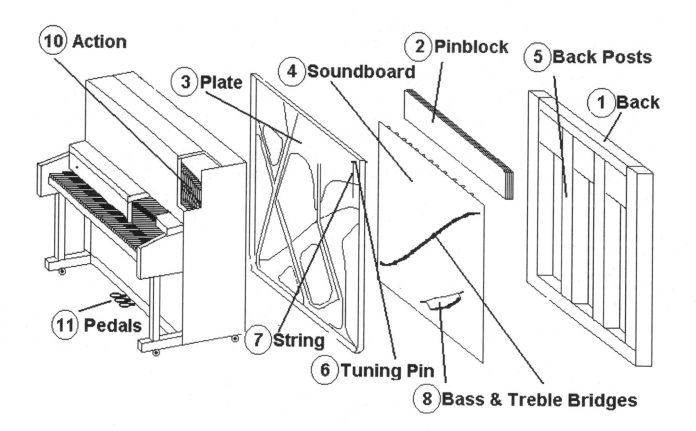

THE SKELETON OF A GRAND PIANO (Drawing 2)

The back or case (outer rim, inner rim) (1) of a grand piano is the wooden frame to which the pinblock (2) is attached, the cast-iron plate (3) is bolted, and the soundboard (4) is glued. It is important that the back posts (5) are well seasoned so that they won't warp. The back and posts help to support about 20 tons of tension. The most common woods used for back posts are poplar, beech, maple, oak, mahogany, and spruce. The rim of a grand is different from the back of a vertical piano because the laminations of wood that form the curved structure are thinner than the back frame of a vertical piano.

In some higher quality and larger grands, most of the posts come together at a point called a tone collector (10), and the sound is redistributed back to the soundboard for more resonance. Some manufacturers believe that the rim of a grand also reflects the sound back to the soundboard for more resonance. However, it is not clear exactly how much resonance the rim reflects back.

The action (10) consists of movable parts that cause a felt hammer to strike the string (7) which is attached to the tuning pin (6). The tuning pin goes through the plate and into the pinblock. The strings are strung on the plate and cross over the bass and treble bridges (8), thus transmitting the sound to the soundboard for amplification. The pedals (14) add expression and sustain notes during performances.

DRAWING 2
SKELETON OF A GRAND PIANO

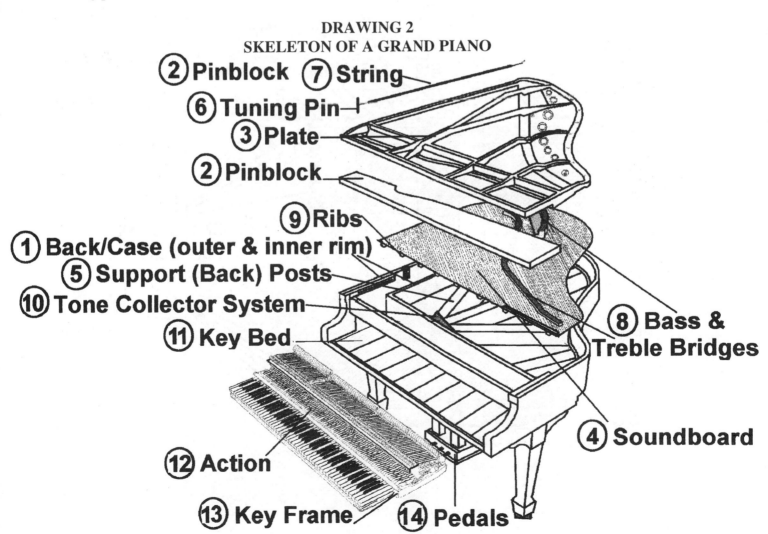

The pinblock (Drawing 1-2, Drawing 2-2, and Drawing 3). The pinblock is a section of laminated hardwood (1) running the width of the back and attached to the back. The pinblock grips the tuning pins (2). It must maintain enough tension that the pins will not slip, thus allowing the strings to slacken and change pitch.

Most pinblocks range from 5 to 40 laminations. Salesmen may tell you their pinblock is better because it has a certain number of laminations, but the number is actually not very important. Pinblocks fail because they are fitted improperly to the back and plate (3), because the holes for the tuning pins have been improperly drilled, or because the wood has not been seasoned properly, not because they don't have enough laminations.

Some manufacturers seal their pinblocks against moisture to help protect them. Such sealing is a decided advantage.

DRAWING 3
THE PINBLOCK AND TUNING PIN

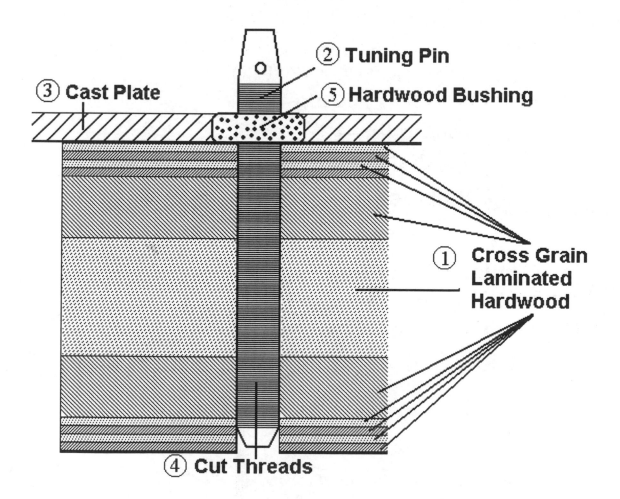

The plate (Drawing 1-3, Drawing 2-3, and Drawings 4, 5, and 6) is made of cast iron and is the primary structure of the piano. Traditional plates (Drawing 4) are cast in wet sand molds and have been adequate for many years. However, a newer vacuum process makes the plate more uniform and eliminates weak spots that have occurred in traditional cast plates. This process is desirable, regardless of whether the design is traditional or full perimeter.

Another variation can be the full-perimeter plate (Drawings 5 and 6). As we would expect, full-perimeter plates support extreme tension much better than the smaller traditional plate, especially if it is coupled with the traditional back support system. However, some piano companies use only the full-perimeter plate and do not use back support posts at all.

DRAWINGS 4, 5, AND 6
STYLES OF PLATES

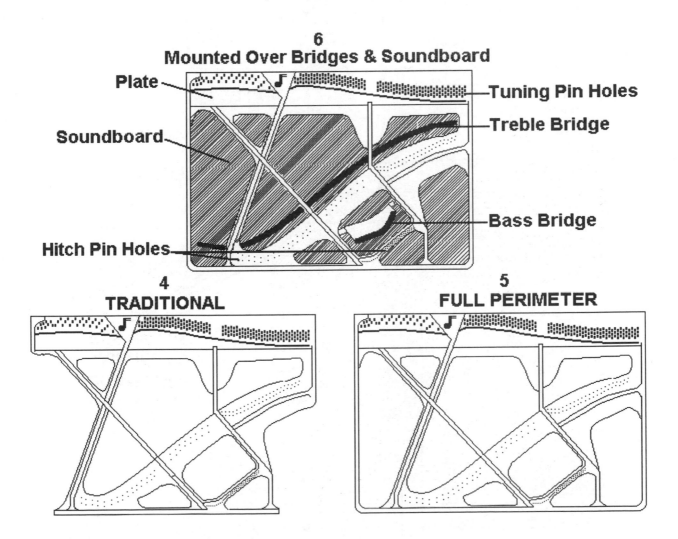

6
Mounted Over Bridges & Soundboard

Plate — Tuning Pin Holes

Treble Bridge

Soundboard —

Bass Bridge

Hitch Pin Holes —

4
TRADITIONAL

5
FULL PERIMETER

6

The tuning pins (Drawing 1-6, Drawing 2-6, Drawing 3) are the steel pegs (2) extending out of the pinblock (1) to which the strings are attached. The technician turns these pins to tighten or loosen the string tension, thus allowing them to vibrate at the proper pitch.

All pins are treated (oxidated, blued) so they will hold better in the wood. Most manufacturers also nickel-plate their pins to retard rusting, a mark of manufacturing excellence.

Pins with cut-thread design (4), which are used by more and more manufacturers, reportedly are less likely to slip because of the angled edge left by the cutting process. I don't know how important this factor is, but I have noticed that it is easier to set the pin if there is more resistance on back turns. I have heard complaints that cut-thread pins grind out the holes and ruin the pinblock, but I have never experienced this problem with cut-thread pins. In fact, some of the higher quality pianos that use these pins seem to tune very nicely.

In most styles, a hard wood bushing (5) surrounds the tuning pin as it passes through the plate. The added thickness of this bushing on the pin helps support it.

DRAWING 3
TUNING PIN

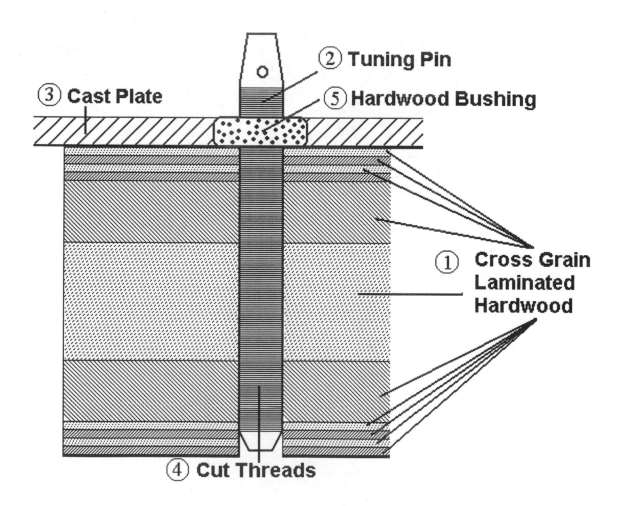

The scale of the piano is the musical part. It consists of the string length in relation to one another, the relationship of the soundboard and bridges to the strings, and the hammers which strike the strings. In short, it is the total musical package of the piano.

Generally speaking, the taller the piano, the better the sound; but check the string length. Some manufacturers put a smaller piano inside a larger cabinet. Others put longer strings and more square inches of soundboard in a smaller package. Usually the manufacturer's brochure will give the lowest bass string length and the square inches of soundboard. However, remember that the length of the longest bass string is only one factor to be considered. You must also consider the height of the piano and size of the soundboard.

The strings (Drawing 1-7, Drawing 2-7, Drawing 7) are different lengths and different thicknesses so that they can be tuned to different frequencies. Fortunately, a thicker string will produce the same sound as a longer one. If all the strings on a piano were made of the same wire and were the same thickness, the piano would have to be almost 30 feet long so that all 88 notes could play in proper pitch. Small pianos use thicker strings in the lower notes than the taller or longer pianos.

All pianos have some distorted harmonics (inharmonicity), and smaller pianos unfortunately have more than larger pianos. Always check the strings for even spacing, even coil windings on the tuning pins (Drawing 1-6, Drawing 2-6, Drawing 3) and equal distance between the coils and the plate.

Some foreign manufacturers string their pianos with a computer-controlled "stringing machine," which is highly accurate but so expensive that many manufacturers do not make enough pianos to justify the cost. These machines put the pin directly in the center of the hole drilled in the pinblock. (When the pins are driven in by hand, they may vary slightly in centering and depth.)

The stringing machines also string the music wire without allowing twists. A twist, even if it is not visible, will create a slightly different vibration that sometimes cannot be eliminated by tuning.

DRAWING 7
THE SCALE AND STRINGS

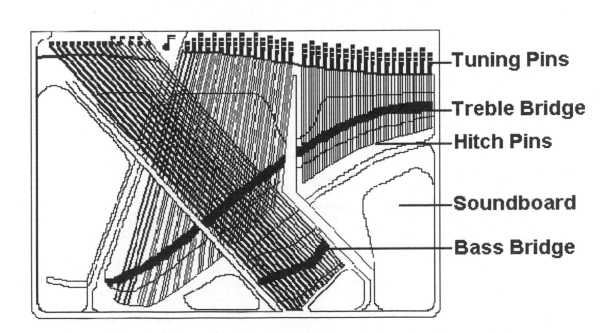

Tuning Pins

Treble Bridge

Hitch Pins

Soundboard

Bass Bridge

Agraffes (Drawing 8) are the best way to space string evenly and are most generally found in grand pianos and provide perfect spacing. Agraffes are best suited for the tenor and bass strings but not in the treble section. In fact, agraffes (1) on all 88 strings may produce a dead sound.

DRAWING 8
AGRAFFES

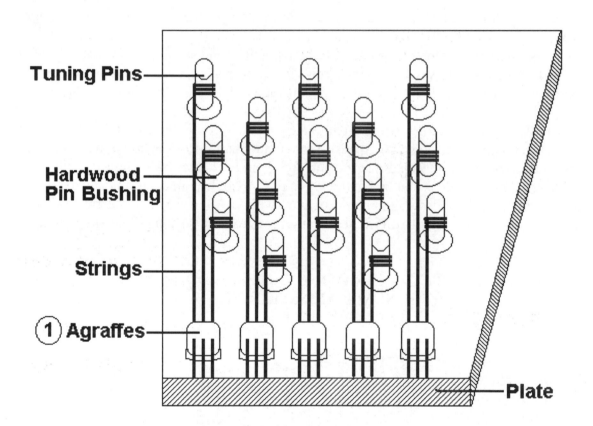

Tuning Pins

Hardwood
Pin Bushing

Strings

(1) Agraffes

Plate

The bridge (Drawing 1-8, Drawing 2-8, and Drawing 9) transmits the vibrations of the strings to the soundboard (Drawing 1-4, Drawing 2-4, Drawing 9). The best bridges are made of maple.

Some manufacturers argue for the superiority of either vertical or horizontal laminations; but the quality of the sound is determined by the quality of the materials and the direction of the laminations is irrelevant.

Bridges need to be accurately notched so that the strings contact the bridge perfectly. Each string of the same pitch must be exactly the same length, a quality assured by the proper notching of the bridge. All piano manufacturers notch the bridge in the treble section; but it is also important to notch the bridge accurately, even in the bass section, if more than one string makes the same pitch.

DRAWING 9
BRIDGES

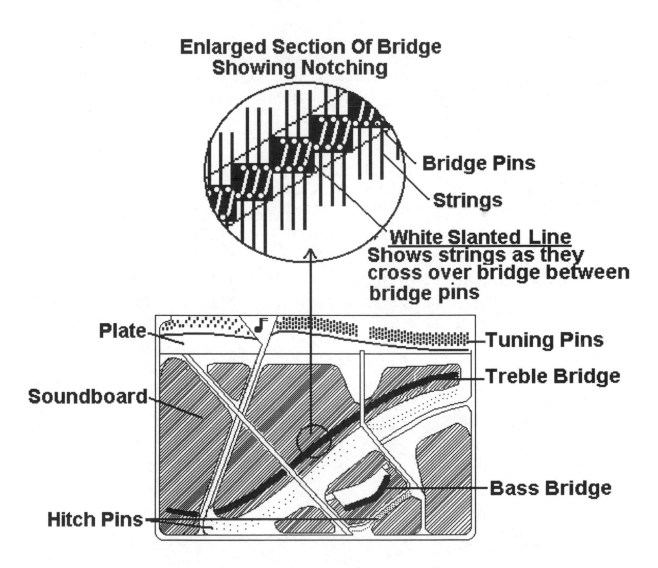

Enlarged Section Of Bridge Showing Notching

Bridge Pins

Strings

<u>White Slanted Line</u>
Shows strings as they cross over bridge between bridge pins

Plate

Tuning Pins

Soundboard

Treble Bridge

Bass Bridge

Hitch Pins

The soundboard (Drawing 1-4, Drawing 2-4, and Drawing 10) is the section to which the bridge is glued. It is the "speaker" of the piano where the vibrating waves of the strings are amplified into the sound we enjoy.

Notice the slight curve on the top (soundboard) of a violin or guitar. This curve is called the crown. This same crown occurs in the piano soundboard. This crown is needed to maintain the downward pressure of the strings against the bridge. The tension created against the bridge causes it to transmit sound better. Without the crown, the half ton of pressure would simply push the bridge away from the strings; the contact would be so slight that only a poor sound would be heard.

The best soundboards are made of quarter-sawn spruce about 3/8 inches thick. Since the spruce boards are only about 4 to 6 inches wide, the boards must be glued edge to edge to create a board wide enough for the piano. Spruce is used in the world's best violins, guitars, and pianos because of its long straight grain. (Grain allows the board's flexibility.) The more grains per inch, the better the board. Check that the spruce is light colored and straight grained. Ask how many grains it has per inch.

Because solid spruce boards can crack, many companies use a board of three or five laminations. Some laminated boards are made of other woods. Others use spruce on the outside layers and another wood in the middle. The best laminated soundboard is one that uses a very thin spruce layer on either side of a solid spruce soundboard. This soundboard or the solid spruce soundboard are best.

DRAWING 10
THE SOUNDBOARD

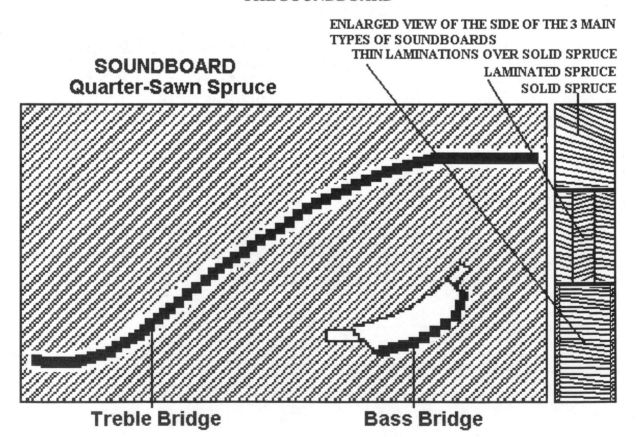

ENLARGED VIEW OF THE SIDE OF THE 3 MAIN
TYPES OF SOUNDBOARDS
THIN LAMINATIONS OVER SOLID SPRUCE
LAMINATED SPRUCE
SOLID SPRUCE

SOUNDBOARD
Quarter-Sawn Spruce

Treble Bridge   **Bass Bridge**

The ribs (Drawing 1-9, Drawing 2-9, and Drawing 11) on the back of the soundboard transmit the sound across the board and help maintain the crown in the board. A high-quality piano will have full length ribs notched into the liner of a vertical piano or the rim of a grand piano.

DRAWING 11
THE RIBS

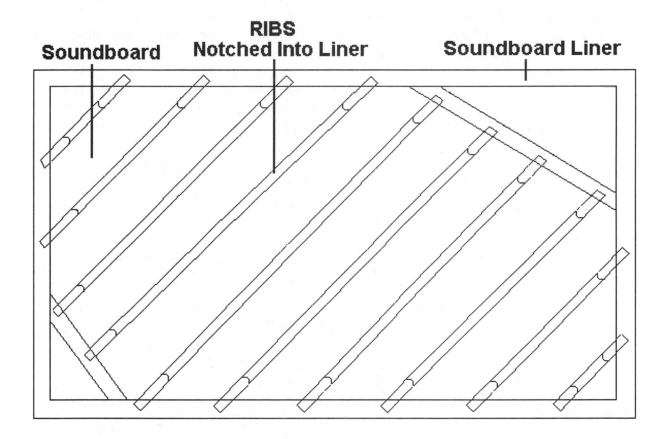

Soundboard   **RIBS**
          Notched Into Liner   **Soundboard Liner**

The action includes all of the movable mechanical parts that, when they function properly, make the hammer strike the string and start it vibrating. The quality of the parts and their functioning determines the quality and efficiency of the action. The main reason for buying a grand piano rather than a vertical piano (assuming that both are good quality) is that the grand's action responds faster and is much more efficient than the vertical's. Many things must happen in any action between the time you push down the key and the time the note sounds.

Here's how action works in a grand piano (Drawing 12). When you push down the key (1), it tilts on the balance rail (2) like a teeter-totter and the back end rises. As it does, the capstan screw (3) pushes up the mechanism (consisting of the wippen (17), the jack (4), and the repetition lever (5). The jack is pushed up through a slot in the repetition lever and presses a knuckle (6) attached to the hammer shank (7). The shank is attached to the hammer (8), which rises toward the string. When the hammer is about half way up, the back of the key contacts the damper lever (10), which raises the damper (11) off the string. When the damper is up, the string can vibrate freely.

When the hammer is about a quarter of an inch away from the string, the toe of the jack comes in contact with the let off button (12) causing the jack to slip out from under the knuckle. At the same time, the repetition lever contacts the drop screw (13), which will rise no further. When the jack and the repetition lever are no longer forcing the hammer up, the momentum of the hammer carries it the short distance left to the string. The hammer hits the string, then bounces back.

The knuckle then falls and rests on the repetition lever, causing the lever to compress against the repetition spring (14). While this is happening, the back check (16) catches the tail (15) of the hammer, holding it in place. When the hammer is barely released, the repetition lever raises the knuckle just enough to allow the jack to slip back under.

The process can now begin all over again as you either repeat that note or play a different one. As long as the key is depressed, the damper will remain off the string but as soon as the key is let up half way the damper will stop the string from sounding.

DRAWING 12
GRAND PIANO ACTION

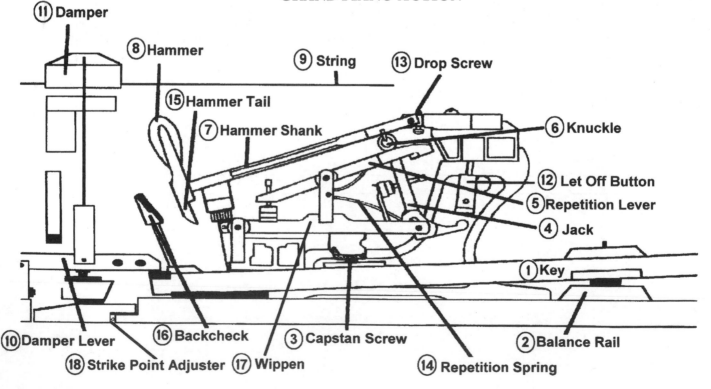

<u>Here's how the vertical action works (Drawing 13).</u> When you push down the key (1), the key tilts on the balance rail (2) like a teeter-totter and the back end rises. When it moves up, the capstan screw (3) pushes up the mechanism, consisting of the jack (4) which is connected to and pivots on the wippen (5). The jack (4) pushes against the hammer butt (6), moving the hammer (7) toward the string. When the hammer has moved half the distance toward the string, a small metal spoon (9) on the back of the wippen contacts and moves the damper lever (10). The lever pushes the damper back from the string, allowing it to vibrate freely. When the hammer is about a quarter of an inch away from the string, the toe of the jack comes in contact with the let off button (12) causing the jack to slip out from under the butt. When the jack is no longer forcing the hammer up, the momentum of the hammer carries it the small distance left to the string. The hammer hits the string, then bounces back. The back check (14) restrains the small catcher (13) on the hammer butt. As the key is released, the hammer returns to its resting position on the hammer rest rail; simultaneously, the jack slips back under the butt and the damper rests against the string to stop it from vibrating.

Then the process can begin again as either the same key or a different one is struck.

DRAWING 13
VERTICAL PIANO ACTION

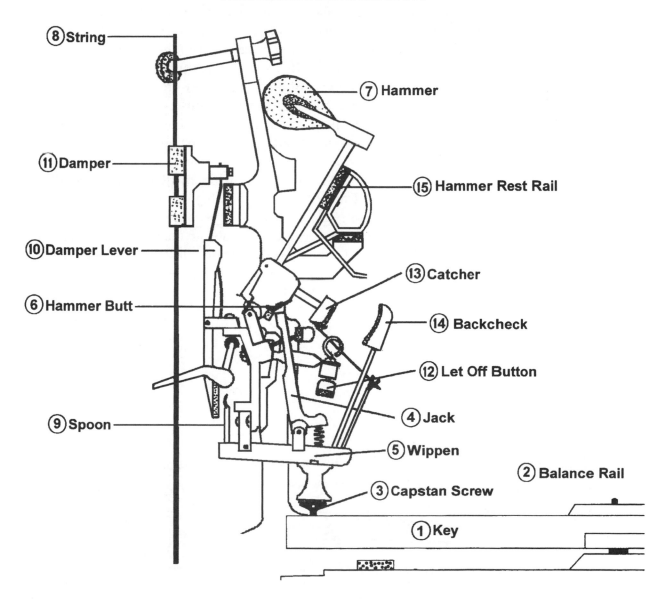

The keys (Drawing 14) are the most visible part of the piano next to the case. Their mechanical and technical quality make or break the performance of even the most skilled artist. They must respond identically to pressure, return at the same speed, and feel identical. Historically, the playing surface of grand piano keys were longer than those of vertical pianos; but piano manufacturers now provide identical playing surface areas on both verticals and grands. This uniformity is a great improvement.

It is important, however, that the key is long enough to provide the proper down weight (the force you have to apply to get the key to go down), the key dip (the distance the key travels down), and the up weight (the force with which that the returning key pushes up against the finger). The greater the length between the balance rail pin (5) and the front, the smaller the difference in down pressure at the front of the key as compared to the back of the key.

High-quality piano makers take great pains to make their keys as rigid and durable as possible. All of the woods should be well seasoned. The grain should be straight and travel the full length of the key for maximum strength. The keys should have hardwood key buttons (7) on the top and hardwood key inserts (8) on the bottom.

A piano key should require about 52 grams of weight on the front edge of the key to depress it. A lead weight (4) on its back, behind the balance rail pin is how the proper weight is achieved. The technician locates the proper position for this weight by sliding it forward until the key starts to move down, then drills a hole in the side of the key and places the weight in it. On a grand piano the weights are placed in front of the balance rail pin. Because of the difference in wood density and the angle the key must make, each key can require a different amount of pressure. This is why each key should be individually balanced and weighted for identical response.

Another important consideration is precise placement of the key bushings and the quality of the felt used in their construction. The friction of the felt against the balance rail pin and the front rail pin must not vary from key to key.

Historically, piano natural keys (11) were made of ivory while the sharps and flats (10) were made of a heavy, dense wood called ebony. Ebony is still used on higher quality pianos, and some grand piano manufacturers use a synthetic ivory for the natural keys; but almost all key tops today are plastic. Concert pianists prefer synthetic ivory because it will absorb the sweat from their fingers and does not get as slippery as plastic. For all but extraordinary use, plastic key tops are perfectly acceptable. Make sure all the keys are spaced evenly apart from front to back.

DRAWING 14
THE KEYS

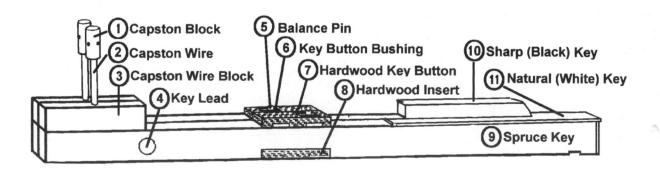

1. Capston Block
2. Capston Wire
3. Capston Wire Block
4. Key Lead
5. Balance Pin
6. Key Button Bushing
7. Hardwood Key Button
8. Hardwood Insert
9. Spruce Key
10. Sharp (Black) Key
11. Natural (White) Key

The <u>key frame</u> (Drawing 15) is the frame on which the keys tilt. The key frame must be made of the highest quality woods to assure that it will not warp, since warping will throw the action out of regulation. The key frame in a vertical piano is screwed down to the key bed. In a grand piano the key frame moves across the key bed when the soft pedal is used and can be taken out of the piano so that the action can be serviced.

The key (9) tilts on the balance rail (21), slipping over the balance pin (5). The balance pin goes through the hardwood key button (7), which is lined with a felt key button bushing (6). This bushing keeps the pin from rubbing directly on the wood and creating noise. The pin then goes through the key and through a hardwood key insert (8). The balance pin is secured in a hardwood insert (23) located in the balance rail. A felt washer called a balance cloth (20) keeps the key from sitting directly on the balance rail and stops it from knocking on the balance rail while the key tilts back and forth during play.

The keys are leveled by paper washers of different thicknesses called balance paper punchings (19). These punchings, which sit on the balance rail, are placed over the balance pin and under the balance cloth. The weight of the action parts lies on the capstan block (1), causing the back end of the key to rest on the key rail (24). A felt rail cloth (23) keeps the key from making a knocking sound when it returns to the key rail.

Playing the key depresses the front end over the front pin (15). The front pin is a lot like the balance pin (5) except that the front pin does not go all the way through the key. A felt-lined notch under the front of the key slides up and down on the front pin. The lining is a front pin bushing (12). Over the front pin and sitting on the front rail (17) is a similar felt washer called a front pin cloth (14) which keeps the key from knocking as it is pushed down towards the front rail. Paper washers called front pin paper punchings (13) level the felt washers so that all of the keys will go down the same distance as they are played.

The corners of the frame should have hardwood inserts (22) so that the frame will not warp. Moisture cuts in appropriate places under the key frame allow the wood to expand in moist climates.

A reinforced key frame pin (16) should be located on grand piano key frames. Usually the pin will go directly into the wood. A reinforced pin is attached to a metal plate that is attached to the key frame. Pressure on the pin is absorbed by the plate and not the key frame, eliminating any damage to the key frame.

DRAWING 15
KEY AND KEY FRAME ASSEMBLY

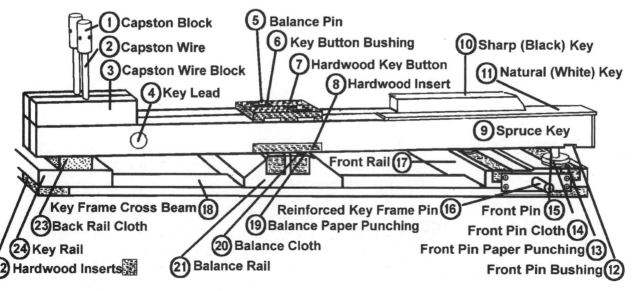

The key bed (Drawing 16) holds the key frame, which is screwed down in a vertical or upon which it moves on in a grand. The key bed (1) must be manufactured with the same care as the key frame. On a grand piano, the key frame must fit perfectly into the piano yet slide out to allow servicing. Hard wood inserts must be added in the corners and along the frame to assure that no warping will occur. Hard wood inserts (3) must also be placed in the key bed to allow the key frame to travel without wearing grooves in the bed. Expansion cuts (2) are made in the key bed of grands to allow for any excess moisture. The strike point adjuster (4) allows the grand action to be aligned and secured in its correct place to create a perfect hammer striking point on the string. The strike point adjuster is located in the bass and treble sections of the keybed.

DRAWING 16
KEY BED

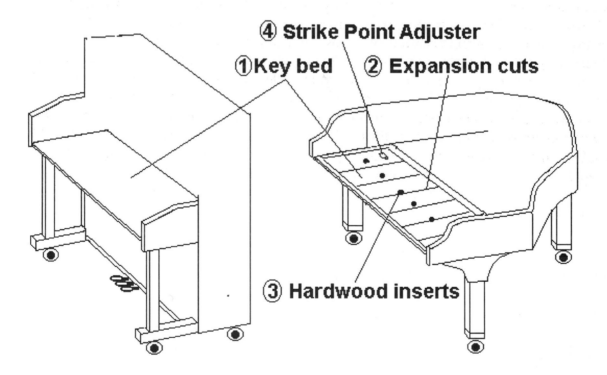

The action is the mechanism that, with the key, carries the hammers to the strings. (See discussion on how the action works for grand and vertical pianos, pp. 12-13). Both materials and manufacturing processes must be very high quality to assure a fine instrument.

Some companies manufacture all parts themselves while others purchase some parts from companies that specialize in their manufacture. I have noticed that a large number of professional pianists choose pianos manufactured with computer-aided equipment in plants that make all of their own parts, right down to the screws. In response to my inquiries, these artists explain that they prefer these pianos because they are highly consistent in how they sound and perform from instrument to instrument while even the same brand of piano from other high-quality manufacturers can vary greatly from instrument to instrument. I am not trying to promote any particular piano, but I think it is to the profession's interest to promote higher quality, speedier responses, uniformity of feel, and greater consistency through every means possible. More manufacturers need to step into the modern age of manufacturing.

The best actions in the world are made of fine hardwoods, like hard rock maple, milled to very small tolerances. Buckskin (or synthetic buckskin) is used for back checks, hammer butts, and knuckles (see Drawings 12 and 13). If buckskin is not used on these parts, the action will be poor in quality and longevity.

Plastic actions are also a new aspect of piano technology. Although plastics have been used in piano actions beginning in the 1950s, those currently available are much better. It is less expensive to produce plastic parts and I expect to see more of this in the future. Time will tell if the performance quality will ever match that of hardwood action parts.

Grand vs. Vertical Actions. Grand piano actions all function generally in the same way, but faster reactions can be produced by various springs, levers, and relationships of the parts. Furthermore, the actions of grand pianos operate differently from those of vertical pianos and are capable of faster repetition and better response than even the best verticals. In short, a good grand action will outperform the best vertical action. If the size of the room in which the piano will be played is not a factor, taller (for verticals) or longer (for grands) is better if the quality of materials is the same.

Vertical pianos (Drawing 17) have different actions according to their size. The keyboards of all pianos are about the same distance from the floor. Because the hammer must strike the string in a precise spot, the action is located differently for each piano cabinet style.

Action 1 is an extended, direct-blow action with full-size parts. The key is connected to the action with a sticker (1) which varies in length according to the piano's height. Manufacturers used to make uprights as tall as 60 inches and used Action 1 in these pianos. However, manufacturers now make uprights no more than 52 inches high, containing Action 2 (full-sized, direct blow). The capston varies in height to make the key come into contact with the action.

Historically, many manufacturers used a direct blow compressed action for console pianos ranging in height from 40 inches to 44 inches. This action had smaller parts and a shorter hammer shank. Because the hammer did not travel as far, it was difficult to get much volume from some of these pianos. Most manufacturers now use a full-sized direct blow action in consoles.

Pianos that use Action 3 are spinets. Although the action parts are full-sized, the key comes into contact with the action very differently.   A sticker (1) below the action is connected to an elbow (2) that pulls the action up. The keys are short with very poor leverage. The actions are very slow, noisy, and difficult to service; the strings are short; and the soundboard is small. It is easy to understand why I do not recommend purchasing spinets; In fact, relatively few are manufactured.

DRAWING 17
TYPES OF ACTIONS

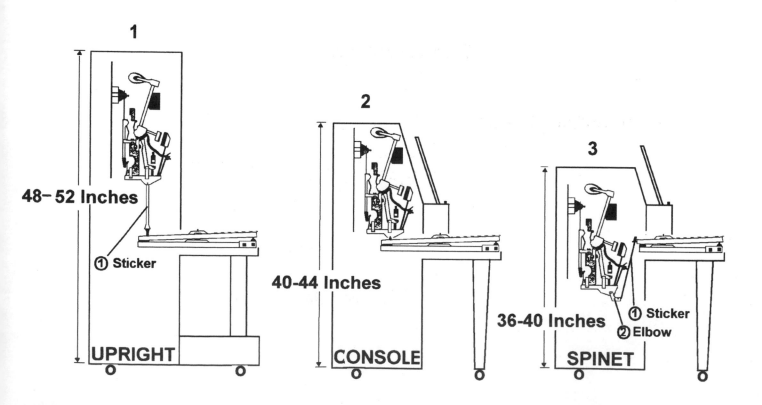

1

48– 52 Inches

① Sticker

UPRIGHT

2

40-44 Inches

CONSOLE

3

36-40 Inches

① Sticker
② Elbow

SPINET

Hammers (Drawing 18) consist of a wooden shank (1) connected to felt-covered mouldings (2). Because the hammer head is the part that actually strikes the string, hammers must be constructed and engineered with the utmost care. They must be capable of playing loudly on one note and softly on the same note immediately, and doing it over and over.

Felt comes in different grades and it is important to manufacturer hammers with the highest possible grade. Discussions of hammer "weight" are not about the weight of each individual hammer but rather about the weight (or density) of the sheet of felt from which the hammers were cut. Usually, the denser the felt, the better the hammer. Concentrate on hammer size before placing a lot of importance on hammer weight. The largest bass hammer should measure 1 1/4 inches or more across the side of the hammer (7).

The under felt (3) is a denser (harder) felt and acts as a buffer between the striking felt and the wooden moulding. Having an under felt is especially important if the outer felt is lighter than 14 pounds. Better hammers have either this under felt or a very dense outer felt.

Another quality check is the stapling (5) that fastens the felt to the moulding. A good quality staple is long. It goes through the felt, through pre-drilled holes in the moulding, and through the felt on the other side, where it is twisted and tied. If the stapling is desk- or staple-gun style, it is virtually worthless. All 88 notes should be stapled.

Ask if a true stiffening agent is used on the top felt (4) to strengthen the hammer. Most manufacturers simply dye their hammers to look as though the felt has been stiffened. Some feel that the stiffening agent is not necessary, but anything that can strengthen the hammer and help it to keep its shape is important.

Next, make sure the hammers are aligned and spaced properly. They should strike squarely all of the strings that are used for each note. Make sure the striking part of the hammers is parallel with the strings. Poor construction or finishing can leave a concave surface.

DRAWING 18
THE HAMMER

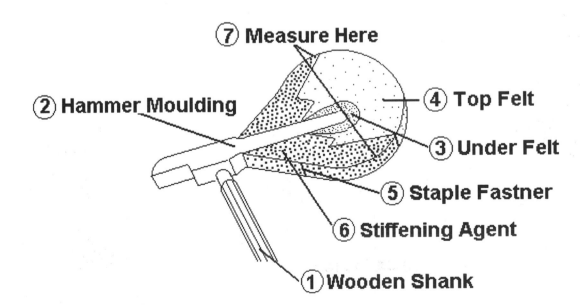

The pedals (Drawing 19) must function as quietly as possible. The construction of the pedals has improved over the years. The pedals should be brass. The better verticals now use tubular steel instead of long wooden dowels and wooden levers. The steel won't warp and needs fewer adjustments.

The sustain or right pedal (1) lifts the dampers of a grand or moves the dampers of a vertical away from the strings to allow the played notes to keep ringing. Some people also call it the "loud" pedal. It can create a little more volume because all of the other strings can ring to sympathetic vibrations when certain notes are played.

The center pedal of a vertical does one of three things (2). First, it sustains the bass end of the piano by moving all of the dampers in this section away from the strings. Second, it can be a practice mute pedal. Depressing it lowers a wide strip of felt between the hammers and the strings, thus muffling the sound. (It usually depresses down and locks to the left so that it can be left on for practicing.) And third, in the best-quality verticals, it is a sostenuto pedal. All of the notes played just prior to pushing this pedal will sustain, while all of the notes played after depressing this pedal do not sustain. Obviously, only the most serious of students and artists need to master this pedal, and only since the nineteenth century has music been written that requires its use. Its presence in a grand piano is a sign of good quality. Some budget grands have a center pedal that, instead of being a sostenuto, is a bass-only sustain.

The left pedal is called the soft pedal (3). In a grand, this pedal, also called "una-corda," shifts the keyboard slightly to the right so that the hammers strike only one of the two strings in the tenor and bass section and two of the three strings in the treble section. This technique cuts the volume quite a bit and makes the sound slightly different. In a vertical, this pedal moves all of the hammers closer to the strings so that they strike the string with less force and, consequently, less volume. It makes very little difference in a vertical piano, however, compared to its effect in a grand.

DRAWING 19
THE PEDALS

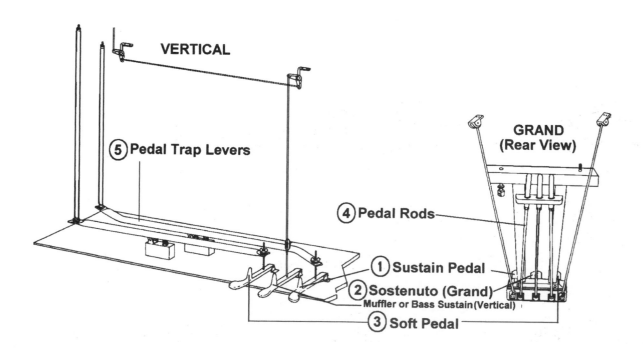

VERTICAL

⑤ Pedal Trap Levers

GRAND
(Rear View)

④ Pedal Rods

① Sustain Pedal
② Sostenuto (Grand)
Muffler or Bass Sustain (Vertical)
③ Soft Pedal

The cabinet (Drawing 20) in the least important but most visible part of the piano. The most important part is the quality of the interior.

Decorators I have consulted recommend simple lines as being less intrusive and more harmonious with many different styles. The least expensive grand piano has a black (polished or satin) finish; wood finishes are more expensive. Color has nothing to do with the sound, but decorators recommend polished ebony grands most of the time because they go with every style and finish of furniture, carpeting, drapes, etc. Most dealers also report selling approximately four black grands to every one of another color. however, some buyers prefer a piano in a particular period style. In general, the more detail, the higher the price. Also, the more hardwoods and solid woods, the more costly.

Some companies manufacture a single quality instrument and install it inside different quality cabinets. Other companies have different grades for different cabinets. If the pianos inside are the same quality, the case has very little to do with the sound.

Signs of high-quality cabinet workmanship are one-piece legs (14) rather than screwed-on legs (13). Legs (8) that are connected and braced by toe blocks (9) are the sturdiest. Hinged rather than sliding fallboards (key lids) (3) are best, since sliding types can become misaligned, damaging the sides of the case. Wood veneer over medium-density board (particle board, pressed wood) is generally less expensive than a solid lumber core, and also has the advantage of not warping. One of the best manufacturers uses medium-density wood in grand piano lids because lids on the prop stick almost always warp if they are made with traditional plywood lumber-core. This company also puts a Formica-type sheet over the board before applying the finish, thus eliminating the grain lines visible in the polished pianos of the other companies. Medium-density board does not affect the sound of the instrument. Just make sure that the veneer is real wood.

Many contemporary manufacturers are switching from lacquer finishes to more durable polyester (plastic) finishes that are easy to take care of.

DRAWING 20
PIANO CABINETS

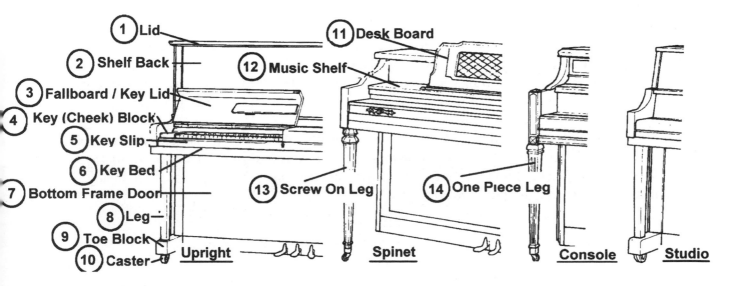

1) Lid
2) Shelf Back
3) Fallboard / Key Lid
4) Key (Cheek) Block
5) Key Slip
6) Key Bed
7) Bottom Frame Door
8) Leg
9) Toe Block
10) Caster
11) Desk Board
12) Music Shelf
13) Screw On Leg
14) One Piece Leg

Upright   Spinet   Console   Studio

USED PIANOS

Factors to be considered in selecting a used piano are:

<u>1. Brand names.</u> Some brand names have excellent and well deserved reputations that are helpful in choosing a new instrument. But there are literally "hundreds" of piano brand names. One that you have never heard of could be a great instrument for your needs. (See the charts at the end of this book for useful information about some brands.) Furthermore, a manufacturer's excellent reputation is of little use when you are choosing a used instrument. If a high-quality instrument has not been cared for properly, it is much less desirable than an average-quality piano that has been serviced regularly. Do not rely on brand name and reputation alone.

<u>2. Antiques.</u> Unlike collectables such as stamps, coins, or antique cars, there are no blue book evaluations of used pianos. Pianos do deteriorate, and the rate of deterioration varies enormously depending on its care. Remember, you are buying this instrument for its musical ability, not for sentimental, investment, or market values.

<u>3. Type.</u> Buy the largest piano you can afford for the space you have available. Pianos with longer bass strings and more soundboard area are better quality if the condition of the pianos is equal. This rule holds true for both grand pianos and vertical pianos.

GRAND PIANOS

The most important reason for buying a grand rather than a vertical piano (if cost is not the deciding factor) is the action. The repetition speed on a grand is faster. Its keys need not be released as high before being struck again. The sound in mid-sized through large grands is usually better and a bit brighter than that of any size of vertical piano.

All 88-key pianos are about the same width, but the length can range from 4 feet 6 inches to 9 feet. Longer is usually better. Even small grands have a better repetition than big verticals, but they may not sound as good. Some Asian pianos are only 4 feet 7 inches, but their strings are as long as some pianos five feet in length. These companies make a variety of sizes up to a 9 foot "concert grand". (Some of these brands are fairly new in the United States and the cost may fit the budget of those looking for used grands.)

VERTICAL PIANOS

If your room will only accommodate a vertical piano, follow the same rule: the longer the string, the better the sound. A large upright (about 48-52 inches), will sound better than a studio (about 44-48 inches), which is better than a console (41-44 inches), which is better than a spinet (about 36-40 inches).

If the condition of the pianos is about the same, the descending order in which I would recommend purchasing a used piano is: (1) large grand (6 feet 6 inches or longer), (2) medium sized grands (5 feet 7 inches to 6 feet 6 inches), (3) small grands (5 feet 7 inches or shorter), (4) large upright, (5) studio, (6) good quality console, (7) inexpensive console, and (8) spinet. Some verticals are better quality than some small grands.

How can you tell if a used vertical piano is good quality? Fortunately, it is not necessary for you to be a piano expert. Consider these six factors. If the prospective piano passes all of them, it is most likely a good piano. If you are unsure, have a qualified technician give you an opinion about the piano's value, quality, and possible problems.

   1. Play each note. Do they feel the same going down? Does each note make a tone. If any of the notes sound as if you are playing two adjacent keys simultaneously, then it may simply mean that the piano is out of tune. If so, a good technician can solve this problem easily by tuning it carefully and regulating the keys. It could also mean that the tuning pins are loose for a variety of reasons. This could spell trouble. It generally means that the pinblock has dried out and may be cracked. If so, it will need to be replaced. This procedure is costly. You should continue your search or you should have the seller have the piano tuned, then try it again and consult the technician before purchasing it.

   2. Check the back of the piano. Make sure the back is glued tightly and that there are no gaps in the frame. Make sure there are no cracks in the soundboard. If you do find cracks, have a technician evaluate their severity before you purchase. Some will make little difference to the sound, but others could be a sign to continue your search.

   3. Check the strings and tuning pins. If they are rusty, the strings could break during tuning. A little tarnish is not important, but a lot of rust usually means trouble.

   4. Check to see that the keys are all level on the keyboard. If some are visibly lower than others, the bushings could be worn out or missing.

   5. Find out the history of the piano if possible. Who owned it? How many owners has it had? Has it been stored? If so, where and for how long? What is its service record? Where was it purchased originally?

   6. What does it look like? This consideration should come absolutely last when you are looking for a used piano. It's fine to want a good-looking instrument; but if it is great and looks great, chances are you'll be paying close to the price of a new instrument. And if you're shopping for a new piano, then you can include the cabinet as one of the factors in your purchase.

   Warranties and service. The best warranty is the one you do not use. Check the reputation of the manufacturer as well as the dealer. There are generally no warranties on used pianos. Sometimes a dealer will include a type of warranty, but it is not from the manufacturer.

   When purchasing a new piano, ask if it comes with a manufacturer's warranty. Most are very good, and most manufacturers will deal with you fairly. Read the warranty carefully. Be sure you understand every item. For example, warranties generally cover defects in workmanship or materials, so it is very important to understand how a given company determines "defect." One company doesn't consider a crack in the soundboard as a defect covered by its five-year warranty. (Five years is not long, considering the life of a piano.) While it is true that small hairline cracks may not affect the sound, these cracks may enlarge, causing great problems later.

   Some parts of the piano may have a longer warranty than others. A laminated soundboard will never crack so a longer warranty should be offered. Make sure the manufacturer will pay for parts and labor. Also make sure that the manufacturer will replace the piano with an identical model or its equivalent at the manufacturer's expense if the defective piano cannot be repaired. Make sure that the exclusions listed in the warranty are reasonable.

   Beware of warranties offered only by a distributor. Some manufacturers make pianos for distributors but do not offer a warranty to the end customer. If the distributor goes out of business, then your warranty is useless. Pianos with a name on them other than that of the manufacturer ("stencil" pianos) are usually not covered by factory warranties.

Ask your dealer about after-sale service. Any new piano has a "settling-in" period during which is adjusts to being moved, the temperature in your home, being played, etc. After a few months, the piano will need some adjustments. One manufacturer offers an exemplary "Servicebond" program that should be industry standard. Rather than just giving a second tuning, the technician goes through a very complete check-off list, which the customer must sign. A reputable dealer interested in continuing service will offer the same kind of program.

How do you locate a reputable dealer? Although most dealers are reputable, they are in business to sell you the piano brands they stock. Their opinions will all be geared to those brands. How long has the dealer been in the piano business in your area? Appraise the variety of his inventory. Have you heard of the brands that he sells? It is better to find a dealer who sells medium- to good-quality pianos rather than one who offers "great deals" in pianos that you have never heard of. (But be aware that some excellent brands are new to this country. The charts at the end of this book will be helpful for some brands.)

As you discuss your instrument needs, appraise whether the salespeople seem knowledgeable and helpful. Are the pianos in good tune and do they play properly? Work your way systematically over the instrument, using this book, and asking questions as you go.

Here are some warning signs:

1. If the dealer does not take the piano apart so you can see everything about the instrument, go elsewhere. You need to see if the instrument you are considering has as many of the features listed in this guide as possible. You do not have to take a salesman's word for it.

2. If the salesman spends most of his time "bad-mouthing" his competition, it is fair to conclude that he does not have a product with many strong points to praise.

CARE OF YOUR PIANO

Ventilation and Temperature

Remember that your piano is made of wood, felt, and leather, all of which are very sensitive to heat (dryness) and moisture. A good rule of thumb is that if you are comfortable, your piano is comfortable. A piano should not be too hot, too cold, too moist, or too dry. Many pianos built today are climitized to the area to which they are shipped, another industry option which should, in my opinion, become a standard.

You may have heard that you should never put a piano against an outside wall. This rule is no longer as important, given modern insulation and heating systems. In a perfect situation, the temperature and humidity around the piano would be constant.

Do not place a piano directly over a heating duct, next to a heat source, or in direct sunlight. If the parts dry out or the soundboard cracks, the piano can become unusable.

Do not place your piano in the direct path of an evaporative cooler. Too much moisture can result in sticking keys, slow action movement, muddy tones, and internal rust. In general, a relative humidity of 50 to 60 percent is ideal for pianos.

Cleaning

Don't place liquids, drink glasses, etc., on the piano that could either can spill and damage the finish or seep into the case. Objects placed on the piano can vibrate, causing an annoying rattle.

Dust can slow the hammer action. Dust the piano frequently with a soft cloth or feather duster. Wipe the finish with a soft cloth. If you need to remove dirt and fingerprints, dampen the cloth slightly, then dry the finish immediately with a dry soft cloth. Wipe off the keys with a soft, dry cloth. Do not use cleaners on the keys; they could damage the finish. If you need to clean extra grime from the keys, use a cloth moistened with a soap-and-water solution. Dry the keys quickly with a soft cloth.

Ask your dealer to recommend a polish if you are buying a new piano with a polyester finish or order the polish listed in the back of this book.

Tuning

The Piano Manufacturer's Association recommends that a piano be tuned at least three times the first year and twice a year thereafter. It should never go without tuning longer than a year.

Regulation, which should be done periodically, is the process of adjusting all of the action parts so they will perform at peak efficiency. Many good technicians spend a little extra time during each tuning to regulate and adjust keys that need it. If the technician does this, you will never have to pay for a separate regulation.

When choosing a technician to work on your piano, DON'T just consider price. You will get what you pay for. Find out some of your technician's qualifications and get references from current clients.

SUMMARY OF WHAT'S BEST IN A PIANO

1. The best pinblocks are made from well-seasoned laminated hardwoods. There should be enough laminations to hold the tuning pin with the proper amount of tension. The pinblock should be sealed against moisture.

2. The best plates are vacuum-processed and, for vertical pianos, are also full-perimeter.

3. The best tuning pins are cut-thread and nickel-plated.

4. The best way to space the strings properly in a grand is to use agraffes. Agraffes should be used in the tenor and bass sections.

5. The best bridges are made of the finest quality maple, well-seasoned and accurately notched so that each string making the same tone will cross the bridge at the proper spot and be exactly the same length.

6. The best soundboards are made of fine-grained, well-seasoned, quarter-sawn spruce. The soundboard should be solid spruce or a sandwich of a thin spruce membrane on either side of the solid spruce board.

7. The best ribs should be full length and notched into the liner of a vertical piano or the rim of a grand piano.

8. The best actions are made of well-seasoned hard rock maple parts with buckskin on all hammer butts and knuckles. The parts should be held in place on metal action rails.

9. The best keys are made of well-seasoned spruce with hardwood key buttons and inserts. They should be individually weighted and balanced.

10. The best key frames are made from the highest quality woods that are well-seasoned to assure against warping. There should be hardwood inserts in the corners and on each key rail. Pins should be secured into hardwood.

11. The best key beds are manufactured with the same concern and quality of material as the keyframe. Since the grand keyframe must move across the grand keybed, there should be hardwood inserts under the keyframe glides and anywhere else the keyframe comes in tight contact with the keybed.

12. The best type of action to use in a vertical piano is a full-sized direct-blow action.

13. The best hammers are made from the finest quality of felt. They should have either a top felt and under felt or have a single dense (more than 14 pound) felt. The staples should pass completely through the top felt, the under felt, the wood moulding, the other side's under felt and top felt, and be twisted to hold there. Individual rests for the hammers are best in grand pianos.

14. The best pedals should be made of brass. All of the trap work and levers should be made from metal to assure that no warpage occurs.

15. The best cabinets have one-piece legs with fully hinged fallboards. Remember that the cabinet is the least important part of the instrument. The quality of the instrument inside is the most important consideration.

16. Check on the service and warranty programs offered by the manufacturer and dealer.

Piano Specifications Tables

This table does not mention all piano brands. The omission of any name in no way reflects negatively on its quality.

The specifications listed come from several sources. Despite every effort to be completely accurate, there could be misinformation in the sources or a manufacturer could have changed the specifications on a particular model. Any inaccuracy is completely unintentional.

BALDWIN VERTICAL PIANOS

MODEL	SIZE & #1 STRING IN.	SQ. IN. OF SOUNDBOARD	SOUND BOARD TYPE	RIBS NOTCHED IN LINER	V-PRO PLATE	FULL PERIMETER PLATE	HAMMER WEIGHT	METAL ACTION RAIL	METAL TRAP WORK
660	43.5" 44-3/32"	1866	SOLID SPRUCE	NO	NO	NO	9	NO	NO
E-100	43.5" 44-3/32"	1866	SOLID SPRUCE	NO	NO	NO	9	NO	NO
2090	43.5" 44-3/32"	1866	SOLID SPRUCE	NO	NO	NO	9	NO	NO
E-250	45" 48-1/16"	1929	SOLID SPRUCE	NO	NO	NO	12.5	NO	NO
243	45" 48-1/16"	1929	SOLID SPRUCE	NO	NO	NO	12.5	NO	NO
5050	45" 48-1/16"	1922	SOLID SPRUCE	NO	NO	NO	12.5	NO	NO
248A	48" 50"	2120	SOLID SPRUCE	NO	NO	NO	12.5	NO	NO
6000	52" 54"	2376	SOLID SPRUCE	NO	NO	NO	12.5	NO	NO

MODEL	TYPE OF KEY MATERIAL	HARDWOOD KEY BUTTONS	WEIGHTED KEYS	CENTER PEDAL FUNCTION	FINISH MATERIAL	STYLES & FINISHES	COUNTRY OF ORIGIN	SEASONED FOR U.S.A.
660	SUGAR PINE	YES	NO	BASS SUSTAIN	LACQUER	3	U.S.A.	YES
E-100	SUGAR PINE	YES	NO	BASS SUSTAIN	LACQUER	3	U.S.A.	YES
2090	SUGAR PINE	YES	NO	BASS SUSTAIN	LADQUER	3	U.S.A.	YES
E-250	SUGAR PINE	YES	YES	BASS SUSTAIN	LACQUER	1	U.S.A.	YES
243	SUGAR PINE	YES	YES	BASS SUSTAIN	LACQUER	4	U.S.A.	YES
5050	SUGAR PINE	YES	YES	BASS SUSTAIN	LACQUER	3	U.S.A.	YES
248A	SUGAR PINE	YES	YES	BASS SUSTAIN	LACQUER	2	U.S.A.	YES
6000	SUGAR PINE	YES	YES	BASS SUSTAIN	LACQUER	2	U.S.A.	YES

BOSTON VERTICAL PIANOS

MODEL	SIZE & #1 STRING IN.	SQ. IN. OF SOUNDBOARD	SOUND BOARD TYPE	RIBS NOTCHED IN LINER	V-PRO PLATE	FULL PERIMETER PLATE	HAMMER WEIGHT	METAL ACTION RAIL	METAL TRAP WORK
UP-109C	43" 43"	1711	SOLID SPRUCE	YES	NO	NO	20.75	YES	YES
UP-118C	45" 45"	1916	SOLID SPRUCE	YES	NO	NO	20.75	YES	YES
UP-118S UP-118E	46" 45"	1916	SOLID SPRUCE	YES	NO	NO	20.75	YES	YES
UP-125E	49" 47-1/4"	2071	SOLID SPRUCE	YES	NO	NO	20.75	YES	YES
UP-132E	52" 49-1/2"	2148	SOLID SPRUCE	YES	NO	NO	20.75	YES	YES

MODEL	TYPE OF KEY MATERIAL	HARDWOOD KEY BUTTONS	WEIGHTED KEYS	CENTER PEDAL FUNCTION	FINISH MATERIAL	STYLES & FINISHES	COUNTRY OF ORIGIN	SEASONED FOR U.S.A.
UP-109C	SPRUCE	YES	YES	PRACTICE	POLYESTER	4	JAPAN	NO
UP-118C	SPRUCE	YES	YES	PRACTICE	POLYESTER	4	JAPAN	NO
UP-118S UP-118E	SPRUCE	YES	YES	PRACTICE	POLYESTER	4	JAPAN	NO
UP-125E	SPRUCE	YES	YES	PRACTICE	POLYESTER	4	JAPAN	NO
UP-132E	SPRUCE	YES	YES	PRACTICE	POLYESTER	1	JAPAN	NO

CHARLES WALTERS

MODEL	SIZE & #1 STRING IN.	SQ. IN. OF SOUNDBOARD	SOUND BOARD TYPE	RIBS NOTCHED IN LINER	V-PRO PLATE	FULL PERIMETER PLATE	HAMMER WEIGHT	METAL ACTION RAIL	METAL TRAP WORK
1520	43' 48-1/4"	2090	SOLID SPRUCE	YES	NO	NO	14	NO	NO
1500	45' 48-1/4"	2090	SOLID SPRUCE	YES	NO	NO	14	NO	NO

MODEL	TYPE OF KEY MATERIAL	HARDWOOD KEY BUTTONS	WEIGHTED KEYS	CENTER PEDAL FUNCTION	FINISH MATERIAL	STYLES & FINISHES	COUNTRY OF ORIGIN	SEASONED FOR U.S.A.
1520	BASSWOOD	YES	YES	BASS SUSTAIN	LACQUER	14	U.S.A.	YES
1500	BASSWOOD	YES	YES	BASS SUSTAIN	LADQUER	14	U.S.A.	YES

HYUNDAI VERTICAL PIANOS (BUILT BY SAMICK)

MODEL	SIZE & #1 STRING IN.	SQ. IN. OF SOUNDBOARD	SOUND BOARD TYPE	RIBS NOTCHED IN LINER	V-PRO PLATE	FULL PERIMETER PLATE	HAMMER WEIGHT	METAL ACTION RAIL	METAL TRAP WORK
U-810	41" 41-1/2"	1799	LAM. SPRUCE	YES	YES	NO	18	YES	YES
U-821	42" 45-3/4"	1898	LAM. SPRUCE	YES	YES	NO	18	YES	YES
U-824	43" 45-3/4"	1898	LAM. SPRUCE	YES	YES	NO	18	YES	YES
U-822	45" 48-3/4"	2075	LAM. SPRUCE	YES	YES	NO	18	YES	YES
J-842 & U-852	46" 48-3/4"	2075	LAM. SPRUCE	YES	YES	NO	18	YES	YES
U-832	48" 50"	2110	LAM. SPRUCE	YES	YES	NO	18	YES	YES
U-837	52" 50-1/2"	2375	LAM. SPRUCE	YES	YES	NO	18	YES	YES

MODEL	TYPE OF KEY MATERIAL	HARDWOOD KEY BUTTONS	WEIGHTED KEYS	CENTER PEDAL FUNCTION	FINISH MATERIAL	STYLES & FINISHES	COUNTRY OF ORIGIN	SEASONED FOR U.S.A.
U-810	SPRUCE	YES	YES	PRACTICE	POLY/LAC.		S. KOREA	YES
U-821	SPRUCE	YES	YES	PRACTICE	POLY/LAC.	2	S. KOREA	YES
U-824	SPRUCE	YES	YES	PRACTICE	POLY/LAC.	5	S. KOREA	YES
U-822	SPRUCE	YES	YES	PRACTICE	POLY/LAC.	3	S. KOREA	YES
J-832 & U-852	SPRUCE	YES	YES	PRACTICE	POLY/LAC.	3	S. KOREA	YES
U-832	SPRUCE	YES	YES	PRACTICE	POLY/LAC.	6	S. KOREA	YES
U-837	SPRUCE	YES	YES	PRACTICE	POLY/LAC.	3	S. KOREA	YES

KAWAI VERTICAL PIANOS

MODEL	SIZE & #1 STRING IN.	SQ. IN. OF SOUNDBOARD	SOUND BOARD TYPE	RIBS NOTCHED IN LINER	V-PRO PLATE	FULL PERIMETER PLATE	HAMMER WEIGHT	METAL ACTION RAIL	METAL TRAP WORK
CX-5	41" 42"	1892	LAM. SPRUCE	YES	NO	NO	16	YES	YES
502-503	42" 42"	1892	SOLID SPRUCE	YES	NO	NO	16	YES	YES
504	43" 46"	1892	SOLID SPRUCE	YES	NO	NO	16	YES	YES
603-604	44" 42"	1892	SOLID SPRUCE	YES	NO	NO	16	YES	YES
CE-11	44" 45.6"	2046	SOLID SPRUCE	YES	NO	NO	16	YES	YES
902	46" 44.9"	2000	SOLID SPRUCE	YES	NO	NO	16	YES	YES
CX-5H	45" 46"	1892	SOLID SPRUCE	YES	NO	NO	16	YES	YES
UST-7	46" 44.9"	2062	SOLID SPRUCE	YES	NO	NO	16	YES	YES
UST-8A &8C	46" 44.9"	2000	SOLID SPRUCE	YES	NO	NO	16	YES	YES
CX-21	48" 45.1"	2093	SOLID SPRUCE	YES	NO	NO	16	YES	YES
AT-120	48" 47"	2155	SOLID SPRUCE	YES	NO	NO	16	YES	YES
AT-170 & NS-20	49" 47"	2155	SOLID SPRUCE	YES	NO	NO	16	YES	YES
US-6X & US-8X	52" 49.4"	2372	SOLID SPRUCE	YES	NO	NO	16	YES	YES

KAWAI VERTICAL PIANOS (CONTINUED)

MODEL	TYPE OF KEY MATERIAL	HARDWOOD KEY BUTTONS	WEIGHTED KEYS	CENTER PEDAL FUNCTION	FINISH MATERIAL	STYLES & FINISHES	COUNTRY OF ORIGIN	SEASONED FOR U.S.A.
CX-5	SPRUCE	YES	YES	NONE	POLYESTER	4	JAPAN	NO
502-503	SPRUCE	YES	YES	PRACTICE	LACQUER	5	U.S.A.	YES
504	SPRUCE	YES	YES	PRACTICE	LACQUER	5	U.S.A.	YES
603-604	SPRUCE	YES	YES	PRACTICE	LACQUER	4	U.S.A.	YES
CE-11	SPRUCE	YES	YES	PRACTICE	POLYESTER	2	JAPAN	NO
902	SPRUCE	YES	YES	BASS SUSTAIN	LACQUER	3	U.S.A.	YES
CX-5H	SPRUCE	YES	YES	BASS SUSTAIN	LACQUER	3	U.S.A.	YES
UST-7	SPRUCE	YES	YES	BASS SUSTAIN	LACQUER	3	U.S.A.	YES
UST-8C &8A	SPRUCE	YES	YES	BASS SUSTAIN	LACQUER	3	U.S.A.	YES
CX-21	SPRUCE	YES	YES	PRACTICE	POLYESTER	2	JAPAN	NO

KOHLER & CAMPBELL VERTICAL PIANOS (MADE BY SAMICK)

MODEL	SIZE & #1 STRING IN.	SQ. IN. OF SOUNDBOARD	SOUND BOARD TYPE	RIBS NOTCHED IN LINER	V-PRO PLATE	FULL PERIMETER PLATE	HAMMER WEIGHT	METAL ACTION RAIL	METAL TRAP WORK
SKV108S	42" 45-3/4"	1897	SOLID SPRUCE	YES	YES	NO	18	YES	YES
KC 043F KC108	43" 43-1/2"	1888.4	* SPRUCE	YES	YES	NO	18	YES	YES
SKV430	43" 45-3/4"	1897	SOLID SPRUCE	YES	YES	NO	18	YES	YES
KC114	44-1/2" 43-1/2"	1888.4	* SPRUCE	YES	YES	NO	18	YES	YES
SKV118	46.5" 48-3/4"	2075	SOLID SPRUCE	YES	YES	NO	18	YES	YES
SKV465 SKV470	46-1/2" 48-3/4"	2075	SOLID SPRUCE	YES	YES	NO	18	YES	YES
SKV48S	48" 50"	2110	SOLID SPRUCE	YES	YES	NO	18	YES	YES
SKV52S	52" 50-1/2"	2375	SOLID SPRUCE	YES	YES	NO	18	YES	YES

MODEL	TYPE OF KEY MATERIAL	HARDWOOD KEY BUTTONS	WEIGHTED KEYS	CENTER PEDAL FUNCTION	FINISH MATERIAL	STYLES & FINISHES	COUNTRY OF ORIGIN	SEASONED FOR U.S.A.
SKV108	SPRUCE	YES	YES	PRACTICE	POLY/LAC.	2	S. KOREA	YES
043-108	SPRUCE	YES	YES	PRACTICE	POLY/LAC	5	INDONESIA	YES
SKV430	SPRUCE	YES	YES	PRACTICE	POLY/LAC.	5	S. KOREA	YES
KC114	SPRUCE	YES	YES	PRACTICE	POLY/LAC	3	INDONESIA	YES
SKV118	SPRUCE	YES	YES	PRACTICE	POLY/LAC.	3	S. KOREA	YES
465470	SPRUCE	YES	YES	PRACTICE	POLY/LAC.	3	S. KOREA	YES
SKV48S	SPRUCE	YES	YES	PRACTICE	POLY/LAC.	6	S. KOREA	YES
SKV52S	SPRUCE	YES	YES	PRACTICE	POLY/LAC.	3	S. KOREA	YES

MASON & HAMLIN VERTICAL PIANOS

MODEL	SIZE & #1 STRING IN.	SQ. IN. OF SOUNDBOARD	SOUND BOARD TYPE	RIBS NOTCHED IN LINER	V-PRO PLATE	FULL PERIMETER PLATE	HAMMER WEIGHT	METAL ACTION RAIL	METAL TRAP WORK
50	50" 48"	2120	SOLID SPRUCE	NO	NO	NO	16	NO	NO

MODEL	TYPE OF KEY MATERIAL	HARDWOOD KEY BUTTONS	WEIGHTED KEYS	CENTER PEDAL FUNCTION	FINISH MATERIAL	STYLES & FINISHES	COUNTRY OF ORIGIN	SEASONED FOR U.S.A.
50	SPRUCE	YES	YES	SOSTENUTO	LACQUER	5	U.S.A.	YES

NAKAMURA VERTICAL PIANOS (BUILT BY YOUNG CHANG, GERMAN (ABEL HAMMERS) ARE USED)

MODEL	SIZE & #1 STRING IN.	SQ. IN. OF SOUNDBOARD	SOUND BOARD TYPE	RIBS NOTCHED IN LINER	V-PRO PLATE	FULL PERIMETER PLATE	HAMMER WEIGHT	METAL ACTION RAIL	METAL TRAP WORK
N-121	48" 43-1/4"	1722	SOLID SPRUCE	YES	YES	NO	18	YES	YES
N-131	52" 47"	1846	SOLID SPRUCE	YES	YES	NO	18	YES	YES

MODEL	TYPE OF KEY MATERIAL	HARDWOOD KEY BUTTONS	WEIGHTED KEYS	CENTER PEDAL FUNCTION	FINISH MATERIAL	STYLES & FINISHES	COUNTRY OF ORIGIN	SEASONED FOR U.S.A.
N-121	SPRUCE	YES	YES	PRACTICE	POLYESTER	3	JAPAN/KOR	YES
N-131	SPRUCE	YES	YES	PRACTICE	POLYESTER	3	JAPAN/KOR	YES

PETROF VERTICAL PIANOS

MODEL	SIZE & #1 STRING IN.	SQ. IN. OF SOUNDBOARD	SOUND BOARD TYPE	RIBS NOTCHED IN LINER	V-PRO PLATE	FULL PERIMETER PLATE	HAMMER WEIGHT	METAL ACTION RAIL	METAL TRAP WORK
100B-105I	42" 39.4	1813.5	SOLID SPRUCE	YES	NO	YES	18	YES	YES
115	45" 41.3"	1906.5	SOLID SPRUCE	YES	NO	YES	18	YES	YES
125-126	50" 43.3	2123.5	SOLID SPRUCE	YES	NO	NO	18	YES	YES
131	52" 44.9"	2185.5	SOLID SPRUCE	YES	NO	NO	18	YES	YES

MODEL	TYPE OF KEY MATERIAL	HARDWOOD KEY BUTTONS	WEIGHTED KEYS	CENTER PEDAL FUNCTION	FINISH MATERIAL	STYLES & FINISHES	COUNTRY OF ORIGIN	SEASONED FOR U.S.A.
100B-105I	SPRUCE	YES	YES	PRACTICE	POLYESTER	3	CZECH R.	YES
115	SPRUCE	YES	YES	PRACTICE	POLYESTER	3	CZECH R.	YES
125-126	SPRUCE	YES	YES	PRACTICE	POLYESTER	3	CZECH R.	YES
131	SPRUCE	YES	YES	PRACTICE	POLYESTER	3	CZECH R.	YES

SAMICK VERTICAL PIANOS

MODEL	SIZE & #1 STRING IN.	SQ. IN. OF SOUNDBOARD	SOUND BOARD TYPE	RIBS NOTCHED IN LINER	V-PRO PLATE	FULL PERIMETER PLATE	HAMMER WEIGHT	METAL ACTION RAIL	METAL TRAP WORK
108P	42" 45-3/4"	1898	* SPRUCE	YES	YES	NO	18	YES	YES
JS-043 108	43" 43-1/2"	1888.4	* SPRUCE	YES	YES	YES	18	YES	YES
SU-143 343	43" 45-3/4"	1898	* SPRUCE	YES	YES	NO	18	YES	YES
JS-112	44-1/2" 43-1/2"	1888.4	* SPRUCE	YES	YES	YES	18	YES	YES
SU-118 147, 347	46-1/2" 48-3/4"	2075	* SPRUCE	YES	YES	NO	18	YES	YES
SU-121	48" 50"	2110	* SPRUCE	YES	YES	NO	18	YES	YES
SU-131	52" 50-1/2"	2375	* SPRUCE	YES	NO	NO	18	YES	YES

MODEL	TYPE OF KEY MATERIAL	HARDWOOD KEY BUTTONS	WEIGHTED KEYS	CENTER PEDAL FUNCTION	FINISH MATERIAL	STYLES & FINISHES	COUNTRY OF ORIGIN	SEASONED FOR U.S.A.
108P	SPRUCE	YES	YES	PRACTICE	POLY U.	9	S. KOREA	YES
JS-043 108	SPRUCE	YES	YES	PRACTICE	POLY U.	5	S.KOREA-USA INDONESIA	YES
SU-143 343	SPRUCE	YES	YES	PRACTICE	POLY U.	5	S.KOREA-USA INDONESIA	YES
JS-112	SPRUCE	YES	YES	PRACTICE	POLY U.	5	S.KOREA-USA INDONESIA	YES
SU-118, 147, 347	SPRUCE	YES	YES	PRACTICE	POLY U.	20	S. KOREA & U.S.A.	YES
SU-121	SPRUCE	YES	YES	PRACTICE	POLY U.	2	S. KOREA	YES
SU-131	SPRUCE	YES	YES	PRACTICE	POLY U.	2	S. KOREA	YES

SCHIMMELL VERTICAL PIANOS

MODEL	SIZE & #1 STRING IN.	SQ. IN. OF SOUNDBOARD	SOUND BOARD TYPE	RIBS NOTCHED IN LINER	V-PRO PLATE	FULL PERIMETER PLATE	HAMMER WEIGHT	METAL ACTION RAIL	METAL TRAP WORK
112-114	45" 46.2"	1736	SOLID SPRUCE	YES	NO	NO	18	NO	NO
116	46" 46.2"	1736	SOLID SPRUCE	YES	NO	NO	18	NO	NO
120	48" 48.2"	1829	SOLID SPRUCE	YES	NO	NO	18	NO	NO
122	49" 48.2"	1829	SOLID SPRUCE	YES	NO	NO	18	NO	NO
130	51" 47.7"	1519	SOLID SPRUCE	YES	NO	NO	18	NO	NO

MODEL	TYPE OF KEY MATERIAL	HARDWOOD KEY BUTTONS	WEIGHTED KEYS	CENTER PEDAL FUNCTION	FINISH MATERIAL	STYLES & FINISHES	COUNTRY OF ORIGIN	SEASONED FOR U.S.A.
112-114	SPRUCE	YES	YES	PRACTICE	POLY/LAC.	4	GERMANY	YES
116	SPRUCE	YES	YES	PRACTICE	POLY/LAC.	3	GERMANY	YES
120	SPRUCE	YES	YES	PRACTICE	POLY/LAC.	11	GERMANY	YES
122	SPRUCE	YES	YES	PRACTICE	POLY/LAC.	4	GERMANY	YES
130	SPRUCE	YES	YES	PRACTICE	POLY/LAC.	3	GERMANY	YES

ADDITIONAL FEATURES: 1-UPRIGHTS CAN COME AS SILENT PINAOS (EQUIPPED WITH DIGITAL SOUND SOURCE)

STEINWAY VERTICAL PIANOS

MODEL	SIZE & #1 STRING IN.	SQ. IN. OF SOUNDBOARD	SOUND BOARD TYPE	RIBS NOTCHED IN LINER	V-PRO PLATE	FULL PERIMETER PLATE	HAMMER WEIGHT	METAL ACTION RAIL	METAL TRAP WORK
4510	45" 43-1/2"	1944	SOLID SPRUCE	YES	NO	NO	12	NO	NO
1098	46.5" 43-1/2"	1944	SOLID SPRUCE	YES	NO	NO	12	NO	NO
K-52	52" 46-3/8"	2088	SOLID SPRUCE	YES	NO	NO	15	NO	NO

MODEL	TYPE OF KEY MATERIAL	HARDWOOD KEY BUTTONS	WEIGHTED KEYS	CENTER PEDAL FUNCTION	FINISH MATERIAL	STYLES & FINISHES	COUNTRY OF ORIGIN	SEASONED FOR U.S.A.
4510	SPRUCE	YES	YES	SOSTENUTO	LACQUER	1	U.S.A.	YES
1098	SPRUCE	YES	YES	SOSTENUTO	LACQUER	2	U.S.A.	YES
K-52	SPRUCE	YES	YES	SOSTENUTO	LACQUER	3	U.S.A.	YES

WEBER VERTICAL PIANOS (MADE BY YOUNG CHANG)

MODEL	SIZE & #1 STRING IN.	SQ. IN. OF SOUNDBOARD	SOUND BOARD TYPE	RIBS NOTCHED IN LINER	V-PRO PLATE	FULL PERIMETER PLATE	HAMMER WEIGHT	METAL ACTION RAIL	METAL TRAP WORK
W-40	42" 40"	1598	SOLID SPRUCE	YES	YES	YES	16	YES	YES
W-109	43" 40-1/4"	1680	SOLID SPRUCE	YES	YES	YES	16	YES	YES
W-41A W-41	43" 40"	1674	SOLID SPRUCE	YES	YES	YES	16	YES	YES
WFX-43	43-1/5" 41-1/4"	1688	SOLID SPRUCE	YES	YES	YES	16	YES	YES
WFD-44	44.5" 41-1/4"	1688	SOLID SPRUCE	YES	YES	YES	16	YES	YES
W-45C	45" 47-1/2"	1848	SOLID SPRUCE	YES	YES	YES	16	YES	YES
WC-46	46" 48"	1848	SOLID SPRUCE	YES	YES	YES	16	YES	YES
WS-46	46" 47-1/2"	2049	SOLID SPRUCE	YES	YES	YES	16	YES	YES
W-121	48" 50-1/4"	1911	SOLID SPRUCE	YES	YES	YES	16	YES	YES
W-48	48" 43-1/4"	1843	SOLID SPRUCE	YES	YES	YES	16	YES	YES
W-53	52" 47"	2074	SOLID SPRUCE	YES	YES	YES	16	YES	YES

WEBER PIANOS (CONTINUED)

MODEL	TYPE OF KEY MATERIAL	HARDWOOD KEY BUTTONS	WEIGHTED KEYS	CENTER PEDAL FUNCTION	FINISH MATERIAL	STYLES & FINISHES	COUNTRY OF ORIGIN	SEASONED FOR U.S.A.
W-40	SPRUCE	YES	YES	NONE	POLYESTER	1	S. KOREA	YES
W-109	SPRUCE	YES	YES	NONE	POLYESTER	2	CHINA	YES
W-41A-WF41	SPRUCE	YES	YES	PRACTICE	POLYESTER	7	S. KOREA	YES
WFX-43	SPRUCE	YES	YES	PRACTICE	LACQUER	1	S. KOREA	YES
WFX-44	SPRUCE	YES	YES	PRACTICE	LACQUER	3	S. KOREA	YES
W-45C	SPRUCE	YES	YES	PRACTICE	LACQUER	1	S. KOREA	YES
WC-46	SPRUCE	YES	YES	PRACTICE	POLYESTER	3	S. KOREA	YES
WS-46	SPRUCE	YES	YES	PRACTICE	LACQUER	2	S. KOREA	YES
W-121	SPRUCE	YES	YES	PRACTICE	POLYESTER	6	S. KOREA CHINA	YES
W-48	SPRUCE	YES	YES	PRACTICE	POLYESTER	6	S. KOREA CHINA	YES
W-53	SPRUCE	YES	YES	PRACTICE	POLYESTER	2	S. KOREA	YES

WEINBACH VERTICAL PIANOS (MADE BY PETROF)

MODEL	SIZE & #1 STRING IN.	SQ. IN. OF SOUNDBOARD	SOUND BOARD TYPE	RIBS NOTCHED IN LINER	V-PRO PLATE	FULL PERIMETER PLATE	HAMMER WEIGHT	METAL ACTION RAIL	METAL TRAP WORK
104-III	42' 39.4"	1813.5	SOLID SPRUCE	YES	NO	YES	18	YES	YES
114-I - 114-IV	45" 41.3"	1906.5	SOLID SPRUCE	YES	NO	YES	18	YES	YES
124-II	50" 43.3"	2123.5	SOLID SPRUCE	YES	NO	NO	18	YES	YES

MODEL	TYPE OF KEY MATERIAL	HARDWOOD KEY BUTTONS	WEIGHTED KEYS	CENTER PEDAL FUNCTION	FINISH MATERIAL	STYLES & FINISHES	COUNTRY OF ORIGIN	SEASONED FOR U.S.A.
104-III	SPRUCE	YES	YES	PRACTICE	POLYESTER	3	CZECH R.	YES
114-I - 114-IV	SPRUCE	YES	YES	PRACTICE	POLYESTER	3	CZECH R.	YES
124-II	SPRUCE	YES	YES	PRACTICE	POLYESTER	3	CZECH R.	YES

WURLITZER VERTICAL PIANOS

MODEL	SIZE & #1 STRING IN.	SQ. IN. OF SOUNDBOARD	SOUND BOARD TYPE	RIBS NOTCHED IN LINER	V-PRO PLATE	FULL PERIMETER PLATE	HAMMER WEIGHT	METAL ACTION RAIL	METAL TRAP WORK
2270 2277S	42" 42-11/16"	1988	LAM. SPRUCE	NO	NO	NO	9	NO	NO

MODEL	TYPE OF KEY MATERIAL	HARDWOOD KEY BUTTONS	WEIGHTED KEYS	CENTER PEDAL FUNCTION	FINISH MATERIAL	STYLES & FINISHES	COUNTRY OF ORIGIN	SEASONED FOR U.S.
2270-77S	BASSWOOD	YES	NO	BASS SUSTAIN	LACQUER	3	U.S.A.	YES

YAMAHA VERTICAL PIANOS

MODEL	SIZE & #1 STRING IN.	SQ. IN. OF SOUNDBOARD	SOUND BOARD TYPE	RIBS NOTCHED IN LINER	V-PRO PLATE	FULL PERIMETER PLATE	HAMMER WEIGHT	METAL ACTION RAIL	METAL TRAP WORK
M450, 600, M1F	44" 44-1/2"	1943	SOLID SPRUCE	YES	YES	YES	19	YES	YES
P2E - MX88	45" 44-1/2"	2016	SOLID SPRUCE	YES	YES	YES	19	YES	YES
P-22	45-1/2 44-1/2"	2011	SOLID SPRUCE	YES	YES	YES	14	YES	YES
U1S	48" 44-1/2"	2137	SOLID SPRUCE	YES	YES	NO	22	YES	YES
WX1S	48" 46.8"	2137	SOLID SPRUCE	YES	YES	NO	22	YES	YES
U3S	52" 47-1/2"	2369	SOLID SPRUCE	YES	YES	NO	22	YES	YES
WX7S	52" 47-1/2"	2369	SOLID SPRUCE	YES	YES	NO	22	YES	YES

MODEL	TYPE OF KEY MATERIAL	HARDWOOD KEY BUTTONS	WEIGHTED KEYS	CENTER PEDAL FUNCTION	FINISH MATERIAL	STYLES & FINISHES	COUNTRY OF ORIGIN	SEASONED FOR U.S.A.
M450, 600, M1F	SPRUCE	YES	YES	PRACTICE	POLY/LAC.	10	JAPAN/USA	YES
P2E - MX88	SPRUCE	YES	YES	PRACTICE	LACQUER	7	JAPAN/USA	YES
P-22	SPRUCE	YES	YES	BASS SUSTAIN	LACQUER	4	JAPAN/USA	YES
U-1	SPRUCE	YES	YES	PRACTICE	POLYESTER	5	JAPAN	YES
WX1S	SPRUCE	YES	YES	PRACTICE	POLYESTER	2	JAPAN	YES
U3S	SPRUCE	YES	YES	PRACTICE	POLYESTER	3	JAPAN	YES
WX7S	SPRUCE	YES	YES	SOSTENUTO	POLYESTER	2	JAPAN	YES

ADDITIONAL FEATURES:1-UPRIGHTS CAN BE ORDERED AS DISKLAVIER (PLAYER/RECORD) AND/OR SILENT (DIG.) SOUND.

YOUNG CHANG VERTICAL PIANOS

MODEL	SIZE & #1 STRING IN.	SQ. IN. OF SOUNDBOARD	SOUND BOARD TYPE	RIBS NOTCHED IN LINER	V-PRO PLATE	FULL PERIMETER PLATE	HAMMER WEIGHT	METAL ACTION RAIL	METAL TRAP WORK
U-107A	42" 40.13"	1603	SOLID SPRUCE	YES	YES	YES	16	YES	YES
E-101	42.5" 40.-1/4	1678	SOLID SPRUCE	YES	YES	YES	16	YES	YES
E-102 E-109	43" 40-1/4"	1680	SOLID SPRUCE	YES	YES	YES	16	YES	YES
U-109C	43" 42-1/4"	1440	SOLID SPRUCE	YES	YES	YES	16	YES	YES
F-108B	43.5" 40-1/4"	1680	SOLID SPRUCE	YES	YES	YES	16	YES	YES
F-116 - U-116S	46" 46-1/4"	1761	SOLID SPRUCE	YES	YES	YES	16	YES	YES
E-118	47" 47.8"	1837	SOLID SPRUCE	YES	YES	YES	16	YES	YES
U-121	48" 43-1/4"	1722	SOLID SPRUCE	YES	YES	YES	16	YES	YES
U-131	52" 47"	1846	SOLID SPRUCE	YES	YES	YES	16	YES	YES

MODEL	TYPE OF KEY MATERIAL	HARDWOOD KEY BUTTONS	WEIGHTED KEYS	CENTER PEDAL FUNCTION	FINISH MATERIAL	STYLES & FINISHES	COUNTRY OF ORIGIN	SEASONED FOR U.S.A.
U-107A	SPRUCE	YES	YES	PRACTICE	LACQUER	3	S. KOREA	YES
E-101	SPRUCE	YES	YES	NONE	POLYESTER	5	S. KOREA	YES
E102,109	SPRUCE	YES	YES	PRACTICE	POLYESTER	5	CHINA	YES
U-109C	SPRUCE	YES	YES	PRACTICE	LACQUER	5	S. KOREA	YES
F-108B	SPRUCE	YES	YES	PRACTICE	LACQUER	8	S. KOREA	YES
F-116 - U-116S	SPRUCE	YES	YES	PRACTICE	POLYESTER	5	S. KOREA	YES
E-118	SPRUCE	YES	YES	PRACTICE	POLYESTER	2	CHINA	YES
U-121	SPRUCE	YES	YES	PRACTICE	POLYESTER	6	S. KOREA	YES
U-131	SPRUCE	YES	YES	PRACTICE	POLYESTER	4	S. KOREA	YES

BALDWIN GRAND PIANOS

MODEL	PIANO SIZE & #1 STING IN.	SQ. IN. SOUND BOARD	SOUND BOARD TYPE	V-PRO PLATE	DUPLEX SCALE	TONE COLLECTOR	DOVETAIL JOINTS	HAMMER WEIGHT	INDIVIDUAL HAMMER REST
MATP2R	5'1" 46-1/4"	1520	SOLID SPRUCE	NO	YES	NO	NO	16.5	NO
M	5'2" 46-1/4"	1520	SOLID SPRUCE	NO	YES	NO	NO	16.5	NO
226, 227 RATP2R	5'8" 48-7/8"	1686	SOLID SPRUCE	NO	YES	NO	NO	16.5	NO
L LATP2R	6'3" 57"	1948	SOLID SPRUCE	NO	YES	NO	NO	16.5	NO
SF10	7"0" 60"	2170	SOLID SPRUCE	NO	YES	NO	NO	16.5	NO
SD10	9' 79-3/4"	2716	SOLID SPRUCE	NO	YES	NO	NO	16.6	NO

MODEL	KEY MATERIAL	DOUBLE NOTCHED BASS BRIDGE	CENTER PEDAL FUNCTION	FINISH MATERIAL	STYLES & FINISHES	COUNTRY OF ORIGIN	SEASONED FOR U.S.A.
MATP2R	BASSWOOD/ SUGAR PINE	NO	SOSTENUTO	LACQUER	4	U.S.A.	YES
M	BASSWOOD/ SUGAR PINE	NO	SOSTENUTO	LACQUER	4	U.S.A.	YES
226 227 RATP2R	BASSWOOD/ SUGAR PINE	NO	SOSTENUTO	LACQUER	6	U.S.A.	YES
L LATP2R	BASSWOOD/ SUGAR PINE	NO	SOSTENUTO	LACQUER	4	U.S.A.	YES
SF10	BASSWOOD/ SUGAR PINE	NO	SOSTENUTO	LACQUER	3	U.S.A.	YES
SD10	BASSWOOD/ SUGARPINE	NO	SOSTENUTO	LACQUER	1	U.S.A.	YES

ADDITIONAL FEATURES; 1-RENNER ACTIONS IN MODELS SF10 & SD10, 2-EBONY WOOD ON ALL SHARPS AND FLATS.

BOSTON GRANDS (MADE FOR STEINWAY BY KAWAI)

MODEL	PIANO SIZE & #1 STING IN.	SQ. IN. SOUND BOARD	SOUND BOARD TYPE	V-PRO PLATE	DUPLEX SCALE	TONE COLLECTOR	DOVETAIL JOINTS	HAMMER WEIGHT	INDIVIDUAL HAMMER REST
GP-156	5'1" 45"	1683	SOLID SPRUCE	NO	YES	YES	NO	20.9	NO
GP-163	5' 4" 47"	1776	SOLID SPRUCE	NO	YES	YES	NO	20.9	NO
GP-178	5' 10" 53-1/2"	2020	SOLID SPRUCE	NO	YES	YES	NO	20.9	NO
GP-193	6' 4" 56"	2284	SOLID SPRUCE	NO	YES	YES	NO	21.6	NO
GP-218	7' 2" 65"	2635	SOLID SPRUCE	NO	YES	YES	NO	21.6	NO

MODEL	KEY MATERIAL	DOUBLE NOTCHED BASS BRIDGE	CENTER PEDAL FUNCTION	FINISH MATERIAL	STYLES & FINISHES	COUNTRY OF ORIGIN	SEASONED FOR U.S.A.
GP-156	SPRUCE	NO	SOSTENUTO	POLYESTER	9	JAPAN	NO
GP-163	SPRUCE	NO	SOSTENUTO	POLYESTER	9	JAPAN	NO
GP-178	SPRUCE	NO	SOSTENUTO	POLYESTER	9	JAPAN	NO
GP-193	SPRUCE	NO	SOSTENUTO	POLYESTER	4	JAPAN	NO
GP-218	SPRUCE	NO	SOSTENUTO	POLYESTER	2	JAPAN	NO

ADDITIONAL FEATURES: 1-SOFT RETURN FALLBOARD

CHARLES WALTERS GRAND PIANO

MODEL	PIANO SIZE & #1 STING IN.	SQ. IN. SOUND BOARD	SOUND BOARD TYPE	V-PRO PLATE	DUPLEX SCALE	TONE COLLECTOR	DOVETAIL JOINTS	HAMMER WEIGHT	INDIVIDUAL HAMMER REST
W190	6' 3" 57-1/2"	1960	SOLID SPRUCE	NO		NO	NO		

MODEL	KEY MATERIAL	DOUBLE NOTCHED BASS BRIDGE	CENTER PEDAL FUNCTION	FINISH MATERIAL	STYLES & FINISHES	COUNTRY OF ORIGIN	SEASONED FOR U.S.A.
W190	SPRUCE	NO	SOSTENUTO	LACQUER	3	U.S.A.	YES

CHICKERING GRAND PIANOS (MADE BY BALDWIN)

MODEL	PIANO SIZE & #1 STING IN.	SQ. IN. SOUND BOARD	SOUND BOARD TYPE	V-PRO PLATE	DUPLEX SCALE	TONE COLLECTOR	DOVETAIL JOINTS	HAMMER WEIGHT	INDIVIDUAL HAMMER REST
410	4' 10' 44-1/16"	1328	SOLID SPRUCE	NO	YES	NO	NO	12	NO
507	5' 7" 48-7/8"	1686	SOLID SPRUCE	NO	YES	NO	NO	16.5	NO

MODEL	KEY MATERIAL	DOUBLE NOTCHED BASS BRIDGE	CENTER PEDAL FUNCTION	FINISH MATERIAL	STYLES & FINISHES	COUNTRY OF ORIGIN	SEASONED FOR U.S.A.
410	SUGAR PINE	NO	SOSTENUTO	LACQUER OR POLY	6	U.S.A.	YES
507	SUGAR PINE BASSWOOD	NO	SOSTENUTO	LACQUER	4	U.S.A.	YES

D.H. BALDWIN GRAND PIANOS (BUILT BY SAMICK)

MODEL	PIANO SIZE & #1 STING IN.	SQ. IN. SOUND BOARD	SOUND BOARD TYPE	V-PRO PLATE	DUPLEX SCALE	TONE COLLECTOR	DOVETAIL JOINTS	HAMMER WEIGHT	INDIVIDUAL HAMMER REST
C142	4' 7" 39-1/2"	1353	SOLID SPRUCE	YES	NO	NO	NO	17	NO
C152	5' 1"	1699	SOLID SPRUCE	YES	YES	NO	NO	18	NO
C172	5' 8" 51-1/2"	1825	SOLID SPRUCE	YES	YES	NO	NO	18	N0

MODEL	KEY MATERIAL	DOUBLE NOTCHED BASS BRIDGE	CENTER PEDAL FUNCTION	FINISH MATERIAL	STYLES & FINISHES	COUNTRY OF ORIGIN	SEASONED FOR U.S.A.
C142	SPRUCE	NO	SOSTENUTO	POLYESTER	5	S. KOREA	YES
C152	SPRUCE	NO	SOSTENUTO	POLYESTER	4	S. KOREA	YES
C172	SPRUCE	NO	SOSTENUTO	POLYESTER	4	S. KOREA	YES

HYUNDAI GRAND PIANOS (BUILT FOR HUNDAI BY SAMICK)

MODEL	PIANO SIZE & #1 STING IN.	SQ. IN. SOUND BOARD	SOUND BOARD TYPE	V-PRO PLATE	DUPLEX SCALE	TONE COLLECTOR	DOVETAIL JOINTS	HAMMER WEIGHT	INDIVIDUAL HAMMER REST
G-50	4' 7" 39-1/2"	1353	LAM. SPRUCE	YES	NO	NO	NO	17	NO
G-80	5' 1" 46"	1699	LAM. SPRUCE	YES	YES	NO	NO	18	NO
G-81-82	5' 9" 51-1/2"	1995	LAM. SPRUCE	YES	YES	NO	NO	20	NO
G-84	6' 1" 54-1/2"	2099	LAM. DPRUCE	YES	YES	NO	NO	22	NO
G-85	6' 10" 61-1/4"	2239	LAM SPRUCE	YES	YES	NO	NO	24	NO

MODEL	KEY MATERIAL	DOUBLE NOTCHED BASS BRIDGE	CENTER PEDAL FUNCTION	FINISH MATERIAL	STYLES & FINISHES	COUNTRY OF ORIGIN	SEASONED FOR U.S.A.
G-50	SPRUCE	NO	BASS SUSTAIN	POLYESTER	5	S. KOREA	YES
G-80	SPRUCE	NO	SOSTENUTO	POLYESTER	7	S. KOREA	YES
G-81-82	SPRUCE	NO	SOSTENUTO	POLYESTER	4	S. KOREA	YES
G-84	SPRUCE	NO	SOSTENUTO	POLYESTER	2	S. KOREA	YES
G-85	SPRUCE	NO	SOSTENUTO	POLYESTER	2	S. KOREA	YES

ADDITIONAL FEATURES 1-REINFORCED KEY FRAME PIN.

KAWAI GRAND PIANOS

MODEL	PIANO SIZE & #1 STING IN.	SQ. IN. SOUND BOARD	SOUND BOARD TYPE	V-PRO PLATE	DUPLEX SCALE	TONE COLLECTOR	DOVETAIL JOINTS	HAMMER WEIGHT	INDIVIDUAL HAMMER REST
GM-1	4' 9" 39.4"	1411	SOLID SPRUCE	YES	NO	NO	NO	18.5	NO
GE-1	5' 1" 43.3"	1597	SOLID SPRUCE	YES	NO	NO	NO	18.5	NO
KG-1A	5' 4" 46.9"	1814	SOLID SPRUCE	YES	YES	NO	NO		NO
RX- 1	5' 5" 47"	1814	SOLID SPRUCE	YES	YES	NO	NO	18.5	NO
GE-2	5' 7" 47.4"	1721	SOLID SPUCE	NO	NO	NO	NO		NO
GE-3	5' 8" 51.8"	1860	SOLID SPRUCE	NO	NO	NO	NO	18.5	NO
KG-2	5' 10" 51.8"	1907	SOLID SPRUCE	YES	YES	YES	NO		NO
RX-2	5' 10" 52"	1907	SOLID SPRUCE	YES	YES	YES	NO	18.5	NO
GS-40	6' 1" 54.4"	2093	SOLID SPUCE	YES	YES	YES	NO		
R-O	6' 1" 55.2"	2062	SOLID SPRUCE	YES	YES	YES	NO	18.5	NO
RX-3	6' 1" 56."	2062	SOLID SPRUCE	YES	YES	YES	NO	18.5	NO
R1-RXA	6' 5" 59.1"	2186	SOLID SPRUCE	YES	YES	YES	NO	18.5	NO
RX-5	6' 6" 59.1"	2186	SOLID SPRUCE	YES	YES	YES	NO	18.5	NO
GS-60	6' 9" 61.9"	2372	SOLID SPRUCE	YES	YES	YES	NO		NO
RX-6	7' 0" 60"	2372	SOLID SPRUCE	YES	YES	YES	NO	22	NO
GS-70	7' 5" 66.6	2635	SOLID SPRUCE	YES	YES	YES	NO	27	NO
EX	9' 1" 79.6"	3255	SOLID SPRUCE	NO	YES	YES	NO	27	NO
GS-100	9' 1" 80.3	3255	SOLID SPRUCE	NO	YES	YES	NO	27	NO

KAWAI GRAND PIANOS (CONTINUED)

MODEL	KEY MATERIAL	DOUBLE NOTCHED BASS BRIDGE	CENTER PEDAL FUNCTION	FINISH MATERIAL	STYLES & FINISHES	COUNTRY OF ORIGIN	SEASONED FOR U.S.A.
GM-1	BASSWOOD	NO	SOSTENUTO	POLY/LAC.	4	JAPAN	NO
GE-1	BASSWOOD	NO	SOSTENUTO	POLY/LAC.	5	JAPAN	NO
KG-1A	SPRUCE	NO	SOSTENUTO	POLY/LAC.		JAPAN	NO
RX-1	SPRUCE	NO	SOSTENUTO	POLY/LAC.	6	JAPAN	NO
GE-2	BASSWOOD	NO	SOSTENUTO	POLY/LAC.		JAPAN	NO
GE-3	BASSWOOD	NO	SOSTENUTO	POLY/LAC.	2	JAPAN	NO
KG-2	SPRUCE	NO	SOSTENUTO	POLY/LAC		JAPAN	NO
RX-2	SPRUCE	NO	SOSTENUTO	POLY/LAC.	10	JAPAN	NO
GS-40	SPRUCE	NO	SOSTENUTO	POLY/LAC		JAPAN	NO
RO	SPRUCE	NO	SOSTENUTO	POLY/LAC.	1	JAPAN	NO
RX-3	SPRUCE	NO	SOSTENUTO	POLY/LAC.	2	JAPAN	NO
R1-RXA	SPRUCE	NO	SOSTENUTO	POLY/LAC.	1	JAPAN	NO
RX-5	SPRUCE	NO	SOSTENUTO	POLYESTER	3	JAPAN	NO
GS-60	SPRUCE	NO	SOSTENUTO	POLY/LAC.		JAPAN	NO
RX-6	SPRUCE	NO	SOSTENUTO	POLYESTER		JAPAN	NO
GS-70	SPRUCE	NO	SOSTENUTO	POLY/LAC.	3	JAPAN	NO
EX	SPRUCE	NO	SOSTENUTO	POLY/LAC.	1	JAPAN	YES
GS-100	SPRUCE	NO	SOSTENUTO	POLY/LAC.	2	JAPAN	YES

ADDITIONAL FEATURES: 1-SOFT CLOSE FALLBOARD ON GS-100.

KOHLER & CAMPBELL GRAND PIANOS (MADE BY SAMICK)

MODEL	PIANO SIZE & #1 STING IN.	SQ. IN. SOUND BOARD	SOUND BOARD TYPE	V-PRO PLATE	DUPLEX SCALE	TONE COLLECTOR	DOVETAIL JOINTS	HAMMER WEIGHT	INDIVIDUAL HAMMER REST
SKG400	4' 7" 39-1/2"	1353	SOLID SPRUCE	YES	NO	NO	NO	18.5	NO
SKG500	5' 1.75" 45"	1675	SOLID SPRUCE	YES	NO	NO	NO	20	NO
SKG600	5' 9.5" 51-1/2"	1995	SOLID SPRUCE	YES	YES	NO	NO	24	NO
SKG650	6' 1" 54-1/2"	2099	SOLID SPRUCE	YES	YES	NO	NO	24	NO
SKG700	6' 10 59-1/2"	2239	SOLID SPRUCE	YES	NO	NO	NO	28	NO
SKG800	7' 64-1/2"	2481	SOLID SPRUCE	YES	NO	NO	NO	26	NO

MODEL	KEY MATERIAL	DOUBLE NOTCHED BASS BRIDGE	CENTER PEDAL FUNCTION	FINISH MATERIAL	STYLES & FINISHES	COUNTRY OF ORIGIN	SEASONED FOR U.S.A.
SKG400	SPRUCE	NO	SOSTENUTO	POLY/LAC.	10	S. KOREA	YES
SKG500	SPRUCE	NO	SOSTENUTO	POLY/LAC.	10	S. KOREA	YES
SKG600	SPRUCE	NO	SOSTENUTO	POLY/LAC.	10	S. KOREA	YES
SKG650	SPRUCE	NO	SOSTENUTO	POLY/LAC.		S. KOREA	YES
SKG700	SPRUCE	NO	SOSTENUTO	POLY/LAC.	2	S. KOREA	YES
SKG800	SPRUCE	NO	SOSTENUTO	POLY/LAC.	2	S. KOREA	YES

ADDITIONAL FEATURES: 1-REINFORCED KEY FRAME PIN ON ALL MODELS, 2-STRIKE POINT ADJUSTER ON ALL MODELS

MASON & HAMLIN GRAND PIANOS

MODEL	PIANO SIZE & #1 STING IN.	SQ. IN. SOUND BOARD	SOUND BOARD TYPE	V-PRO PLATE	DUPLEX SCALE	TONE COLLECTOR	DOVETAIL JOINTS	HAMMER WEIGHT	INDIVIDUAL HAMMER REST
A	5"8" 52-1/2"	2230	SOLID SPRUCE	NO	YES	NO	NO	16	NO
BB	7" 59-3/8"	2726	SOLID SPRUCE	NO	YES	NO	NO	1`8	NO

MODEL	KEY MATERIAL	DOUBLE NOTCHED BASS BRIDGE	CENTER PEDAL FUNCTION	FINISH MATERIAL	STYLES & FINISHES	COUNTRY OF ORIGIN	SEASONED FOR U.S.A.
A	SPRUCE	NO	SOSTENUTO	LACQUER	5	U.S.A.	YES
BB	SPRUCE	NO	SOSTENUTO	LACQUER	5	U.S.A.	YES

NAKAMURA GRAND PIANOS (MADE BY YOUNG CHANG USING ABEL HAMMERS)

MODEL	PIANO SIZE & #1 STING IN.	SQ. IN. SOUND BOARD	SOUND BOARD TYPE	V-PRO PLATE	DUPLEX SCALE	TONE COLLECTOR	DOVETAIL JOINTS	HAMMER WEIGHT	INDIVIDUAL HAMMER REST
N185	5' 2" 45"	1632	SOLID SPRUCE	YES	YES	NO	NO	19	YES
N-157	6' 1" 54-1/2"	2101	SOLID SPRUCE	YES	YES	NO	NO	19	YES

MODEL	KEY MATERIAL	DOUBLE NOTCHED BASS BRIDGE	CENTER PEDAL FUNCTION	FINISH MATERIAL	STYLES & FINISHES	COUNTRY OF ORIGIN	SEASONED FOR U.S.A.
N185	SPRUCE	NO	SOSTENUTO	POLYESTER	5	S. KOREA	YES
N-157	SPRUCE	NO	SOSTENUTO	POLYESTER	6	S. KOREA	YES

PETROF GRAND PIANOS

MODEL	PIANO SIZE & #1 STING IN.	SQ. IN. SOUND BOARD	SOUND BOARD TYPE	V-PRO PLATE	DUPLEX SCALE	TONE COLLECTOR	DOVETAIL JOINTS	HAMMER WEIGHT	INDIVIDUAL HAMMER REST
V	5' 3" 42.3"	1798	SOLID SPRUCE	NO	NO	NO	NO	18	NO
IV-1VC	5' 8" 49.6	1997	SOLID SPRUCE	NO	NO	NO	NO	18	NO
III-M	6' 4" 55-1/2"	2338	SOLID SPRUCE	NO	NO	NO	NO	20	NO
II	7' 9" 67.3"	2807	SOLID SPRUCE	NO	NO	NO	NO	20	NO
I-M.	9' 2" 80.9"	3445	SOLID SPRUCE	NO	NO	NO	NO	20	NO

MODEL	KEY MATERIAL	DOUBLE NOTCHED BASS BRIDGE	CENTER PEDAL FUNCTION	FINISH MATERIAL	STYLES & FINISHES	COUNTRY OF ORIGIN	SEASONED FOR U.S.A.
V	SPRUCE	NO	SOSTENUTO	POLYESTER	4	CZECH R.	YES
IV-IVC	SPRUCE	NO	SOSTENUTO	POLYESTER	4	CZECH R	YES
III-M	SPRUCE	NO	SOSTENUTO	POLYESTER	4	CZECH R.	YES
II	SPRUCE	NO	SOSTENUTO	POLYESTER	2	CZECH R.	YES
I-M.	SPRUCE	NO	SOSTENUTO	POLYESTER	2	CZECH R.	YES

SAMICK GRAND PIANOS

MODEL	PIANO SIZE & #1 STING IN.	SQ. IN. SOUND BOARD	SOUND BOARD TYPE	V-PRO PLATE	DUPLEX SCALE	TONE COLLECTOR	DOVETAIL JOINTS	HAMMER WEIGHT	INDIVIDUAL HAMMER REST
SG-150C	4' 11-1/2" 42-7/8"	1526	* SPRUCE	YES	YES	NO	NO	20	NO
SG-161	5' 3-1/2" 47.625"	1707.3	* SPRUCE	YES	YES	NO	NO	20	NO
SG-172	5' 7" 51-1/2"	1825	* SPRUCE	YES	YES	NO	NO	22	NO
SG-185 WSG-185	6' 1" 54-1/2"	2099	* SPRUCE	YES	YES	NO	NO	24	NO
WSG-205	6' 9" 61-1/4"	2239	* SPRUCE	YES	NO	NO	NO	26	NO
WSG-225	7' 4" 67-3/4""	2569	* SPRUCE	YES	NO	NO	NO	28	NO
WSG-275	9' 0" 82-7/8"	3269	* SPRUCE	YES	NO	NO	NO	30	NO

MODEL	KEY MATERIAL	DOUBLE NOTCHED BASS BRIDGE	CENTER PEDAL FUNCTION	FINISH MATERIAL	STYLES & FINISHES	COUNTRY OF ORIGIN	SEASONED FOR U.S.A.
SG-150C	SPRUCE	NO	SOSTENUTO	POLYESTER	10	S. KOREA	YES
SG-161	SPRUCE	NO	SOSTENUTO	POLYESTER	10	S. KOREA	YES
SG-172	SPRUCE	NO	SOSTENUTO	POLYESTER	10	S. KOREA	YES
WSG-185	SPRUCE	NO	SOSTENUTO	POLYESTER	2	S. KOREA	YES
WSG-205	SPRUCE	NO	SOSTENUTO	POLYESTER	2	S. KOREA	YES
WSG-225	SPRUCE	NO	SOSTENUTO	POLYESTER	2	S. KOREA	YES
WSG-275	SPRUCE	NO	SOSTENUTO	POLYESTER	2	S. KOREA	YES

ADDITIONAL FEATURES 1-REINFORCED KEY FRAME PIN, 2-* SAMICK USES A THIN MEMBRANE OF SPRUCE ON EITHER SIDE OF A SOLID SPRUCE SOUNDBOARD. THIS IS AN EXCELLENT SOUNDBOARD . ALL WSG GRANDS USE A RENNER ACTION.

SCHIMMEL GRAND PIANOS

MODEL	PIANO SIZE & #1 STING IN.	SQ. IN. SOUND BOARD	SOUND BOARD TYPE	V-PRO PLATE	DUPLEX SCALE	TONE COLLECTOR	DOVETAIL JOINTS	HAMMER WEIGHT	INDIVIDUAL HAMMER REST
SC-150	5' 1" 45.6"	1519	SOLID SPRUCE	NO	NO	NO	YES	18	NO
SG-174	5' 10" 51.7"	1674	SOLID SPRUCE	NO	NO	NO	YES	18	NO
SP-182	6"				NO	NO	YES	18	NO
CC-208	6' 10" 59"	1968.5"	SOLID SPRUCE	NO	NO	NO	YES	18	NO
CO-256	8' 4" 75.8"	3208.5	SOLID SPRUCE	NO	YES	NO	YES	18	NO

MODEL	KEY MATERIAL	DOUBLE NOTCHED BASS BRIDGE	CENTER PEDAL FUNCTION	FINISH MATERIAL	STYLES & FINISHES	COUNTRY OF ORIGIN	SEASONED FOR U.S.A.
SC-150	SPRUCE	NO	SOSTENUTO	POLY/LAC.		GERMANY	YES
SG-174	SPRUCE	NO	SOSTENUTO	POLY/LAC.	11	GERMANY	YES
SP-182	SPRUCE	NO	SOSTENUTO	POLY/LAC.		GERMANY	YES
CC-208	SPRUCE	NO	SOSTENUTO	POLY/LAC.	5	GERMANY	YES
CO-256	SPRUCE	NO	SOSTENUTO	POLY/LAC.	2	GERMANY	YES

ADDITIONAL FEATURES: 1-PIANOS CAN BE ORDERED AS SILENT PIANO (EQUIPPED WITH DIGITAL SOUND SOURCE)

STEINWAY GRAND PIANOS

MODEL	PIANO SIZE & #1 STING IN.	SQ. IN. SOUND BOARD	SOUND BOARD TYPE	V-PRO PLATE	DUPLEX SCALE	TONE COLLECTOR	DOVETAIL JOINTS	HAMMER WEIGHT	INDIVIDUAL HAMMER REST
S	5' 1" 45-1/2"	1659	SOLID SPRUCE	NO	YES	NO	NO	16	YES
M	5' 7" 49-1/4"	1816	SOLID SPRUCE	NO	YES	NO	NO	16	YES
L	5' 10-1/2" 54-1/4"	2002	SOLID SPRUCE	NO	YES	NO	NO	16	YES
B	6' 10-1/2" 59-1/4"	2271	SOLID SPRUCE	NO	YES	YES	NO	16	YES
D	8' 11-3/4" 79-1/4"	3245	SOLID SPRUCE	NO	YES	YES	NO	18	YES

MODEL	KEY MATERIAL	DOUBLE NOTCHED BASS BRIDGE	CENTER PEDAL FUNCTION	FINISH MATERIAL	STYLES & FINISHES	COUNTRY OF ORIGIN	SEASONED FOR U.S.A.
S	SPRUCE	NO	SOSTENUTO	LACQUER	3	U.S.A.	YES
M	SPRUCE	NO	SOSTENUTO	LACQUER	3	U.S.A.	YES
L	SPRUCE	NO	SOSTENUTO	LACQUER	3	U.S.A.	YES
B	SPRUCE	NO	SOSTENUTO	LACQUER	3	U.S.A.	YES
D	SPRUCE	NO	SOSTENUTO	LACQUER	2	U.S.A.	YES

WEBER GRAND PIANOS (MADE BY YOUNG CHANG)

MODEL	PIANO SIZE & #1 STING IN.	SQ. IN. SOUND BOARD	SOUND BOARD TYPE	V-PRO PLATE	DUPLEX SCALE	TONE COLLECTOR	DOVETAIL JOINTS	HAMMER WEIGHT	INDIVIDUAL HAMMER REST
WG-50	4' 11" 42-1/8"	1560	SOLID SPRUCE	YES	NO	NO	YES	18	NO
WG-51	5' 1" 43-3/4"	1627	SOLID SPRUCE	YES	YES	NO	YES	18	NO
WG-57	5' 7" 49"	1838	SOLID SPRUCE	YES	YES	YES	YES	18	NO
WG-60	6' 1" 54-1/2"	2093	SOLID SPRUCE	YES	YES	YES	YES	18	YES
WG-70	7' 59"	2376	SOLID SPRUCE	YES	YES	YES	YES	24	YES
WG-90	8' 11" 79-1/2"	3451	SOLID SPRUCE	NO	YES	YES	YES	24	YES

MODEL	KEY MATERIAL	DOUBLE NOTCHED BASS BRIDGE	CENTER PEDAL FUNCTION	FINISH MATERIAL	STYLES & FINISHES	COUNTRY OF ORIGIN	SEASONED FOR U.S.A.
WG-50	SPRUCE	NO	SOSTENUTO	POLYESTER	11	S. KOREA	YES
WG-51	SPRUCE	NO	SOSTENUTO	POLYESTER	8	S. KOREA	YES
WG-57	SPRUCE	NO	SOSTENUTO	POLYESTER	8	S. KOREA	YES
WG-60	SPRUCE	NO	SOSTENUTO	POLYESTER	3	S. KOREA	YES
WG-70	SPRUCE	NO	SOSTENUTO	POLYESTER	2	S. KOREA	YES
WG-90	SPRUCE	NO	SOSTENUTO	POLYESTER	2	S. KOREA	YES

ADDITIONAL FEATURES: 1-REINFORCED KEY FRAME GUIDE, 2-STRIKE POINT ADJUSTER

WEINBACH GRAND PIANOS (MADE BY PETROF)

MODEL	PIANO SIZE & #1 STING IN.	SQ. IN. SOUND BOARD	SOUND BOARD TYPE	V-PRO PLATE	DUPLEX SCALE	TONE COLLECTOR	DOVETAIL JOINTS	HAMMER WEIGHT	INDIVIDUAL HAMMER REST
C-143	5' 3" 39-1/2"	1798	SOLID SPRUCE	NO	NO	NO	NO	18	NO
C-153	5' 8" 49.6"	1997	SOLID SPRUCE	NO	NO	NO	NO	18	NO
C-192	6' 4" 55-1/2"	2238	SOLID SPRUCE	NO	NO	NO	NO	20	NO

MODEL	KEY MATERIAL	DOUBLE NOTCHED BASS BRIDGE	CENTER PEDAL FUNCTION	FINISH MATERIAL	STYLES & FINISHES	COUNTRY OF ORIGIN	SEASONED FOR U.S.A.
C-143	SPRUCE	NO	SOSTENUTO	POLYESTER	4	CZECH R.	YES
C-153	SPRUCE	NO	SOSTENUTO	POLYESTER	4	CZECH R.	YES
C-192	SPRUCE	NO	SOSTENUTO	POLYESTER	4	CZECH R.	YES

WURLITZER (MADE BY SAMICK FOR BALDWIN. BALDWIN OWNS WURLITZER)

MODEL	PIANO SIZE & #1 STING IN.	SQ. IN. SOUND BOARD	SOUND BOARD TYPE	V-PRO PLATE	DUPLEX SCALE	TONE COLLECTOR	DOVETAIL JOINTS	HAMMER WEIGHT	INDIVIDUAL HAMMER REST
C-143	4' 7" 39-1/2"	1435	SOLID SPRUCE	YES	NO	NO	NO	17	NO
C-153	5' 1" 45-1/4"	1699	SOLID SPRUCE	YES	YES	NO	NO	18	NO
C-173	5' 9" 51-1/2"	1825	SOLID SPRUCE	YES	YES	NO	NO	18	NO

MODEL	KEY MATERIAL	DOUBLE NOTCHED BASS BRIDGE	CENTER PEDAL FUNCTION	FINISH MATERIAL	STYLES & FINISHES	COUNTRY OF ORIGIN	SEASONED FOR U.S.A.
C-143	SPRUCE	NO	BASS SUS.	POLYESTER	5	S. KOREA	YES
C-153	SPRUCE	NO	SOSTENUTO	POLYESTER	7	S. KOREA	YES
C-173	SPRUCE	NO	SOSTENUTO	POLYESTER	4	S. KOREA	YES

YAMAHA GRAND PIANOS

MODEL	PIANO SIZE & #1 STING IN.	SQ. IN. SOUND BOARD	SOUND BOARD TYPE	V-PRO PLATE	DUPLEX SCALE	TONE COLLECTOR	DOVETAIL JOINTS	HAMMER WEIGHT	INDIVIDUAL HAMMER REST
GH1-B	5' 3" 45.8"	1670	SOLID SPRUCE	YES	NO	NO	NO	14	YES
C1	5' 3" 46.5"	1742.9	SOLID SPRUCE	YES	YES	YES	YES	17.5	YES
C2	5' 8" 49.8"	1860	SOLID SPRUCE	YES	YES	YES	YES	17.5	YES
C3	6' 1" 56.2"	2062	SOLID SPRUCE	YES	YES	YES	YES	22	YES
C5	6' 7" 59.1"	2201	SOLID SPRUCE	YES	YES	YES	YES	22	YES
C6	6' 11" 61.5"	2434	SOLID SPRUCE	YES	YES	YES	YES	22	YES
C7	7' 6" 66.2"	2666	SOLID SPRUCE	YES	YES	YES	YES	24	YES
S4	6' 3" 57.1"	2093	SOLID SPRUCE	YES	YES	YES	YES	26.6	YES
S6	6' 11" 61.5	2434	SOLID SPRUCE	YES	YES	YES	YES	26.6	YES
CFIIIS	9' 79.9"	3209	SOLID SPRUCE	NO	YES	YES	YES	24	YES

MODEL	KEY MATERIAL	DOUBLE NOTCHED BASS BRIDGE	CENTER PEDAL FUNCTION	FINISH MATERIAL	STYLES & FINISHES	COUNTRY OF ORIGIN	SEASONED FOR U.S.A.
GHI-B	SPRUCE	YES	BASS SUS.	POLYESTER	7	JAPAN	YES
C1	SPRUCE	YES	SOSTENUTO	POLYESTER	7	JAPAN	YES
C2	SPRUCE	YES	SOSTENUTO	POLYESTER	8	JAPAN	YES
C3	SPRUCE	YES	SOSTENUTO	POLYESTER	5	JAPAN	YES
C5	SPRUCE	YES	SOSTENUTO	POLYESTER	3	JAPAN	YES
C6	SPRUCE	YES	SOSTENUTO	POLYESTER	2	JAPAN	YES
C7	SPRUCE	YES	SOSTENUTO	POLYESTER	2	JAPAN	YES
S4	SPRUCE	YES	SOSTENUTO	POLYESTER	1	JAPAN	YES
S6	SPRUCE	YES	SOSTENUTO	POLYESTER	1	JAPAN	YES
CFIIIS	SPRUCE	YES	SOSTENUTO	POLYESTER	1	JAPAN	YES

ADDITIONAL FEATURES: 1- SOFT-CLOSE FALLBOARD, 2 - RESIN SURFACE SHEET BEFORE FINISH, 3- IVORITE AND W.P.C. KEYS ON ALL MODELS C3 AND ABOVE (CF HAS EBONY), 4-REINFORCED KEY FRAME PIN, 5-STRIKE POINT ADJUSTER, 6-ADJUSTABLE PLATE MOUNTING SYSTEM, 7- ANY MODEL CAN BE A DISKLAVIER.

YOUNG CHANG GRAND PIANOS

MODEL	PIANO SIZE & #1 STING IN.	SQ. IN. SOUND BOARD	SOUND BOARD TYPE	V-PRO PLATE	DUPLEX SCALE	TONE COLLECTOR	DOVETAIL JOINTS	HAMMER WEIGHT	INDIVIDUAL HAMMER REST
G-150	4' 11" 45"	1526	SOLID SPRUCE	YES	YES	NO	YES	19	NO
G-157	5' 2" 45"	1632	SOLID SPRUCE	YES	YES	NO	YES	19	NO
G-175	5' 9" 51-1/4"	1841	SOLID SPRUCE	YES	YES	YES	YES	19	NO
G-185	6' 1" 54-1/2"	2101	SOLID SPRUCE	YES	YES	YES	YES	19	YES
G-208	6' 10" 59-1/4"	2304	SOLID SPRUCE	YES	YES	YES	YES	23	YES
G-213	7" 59"	2321	SOLID SPRUCE	YES	YES	YES	YES	23	YES
G-275	9' 79-1/2"	3451	SOLID SPRUCE	YES	YES	YES	YES	23	YES

MODEL	KEY MATERIAL	DOUBLE NOTCHED BASS BRIDGE	CENTER PEDAL FUNCTION	FINISH MATERIAL	STYLES & FINISHES	COUNTRY OF ORIGIN	SEASONED FOR U.S.A.
G-150	SPRUCE	NO	SOSTENUTO	POLYESTER	13	S. KOREA	YES
G-157	SPRUCE	NO	SOSTENUTO	POLYESTER	8	S. KOREA	YES
G-175	SPRUCE	NO	SOSTENUTO	POLYESTER	8	S. KOREA	YES
G-185	SPRUCE	NO	SOSTENUTO	POLYESTER	5	S. KOREA	YES
G-208	SPRUCE	NO	SOSTENUTO	POLYESTER	1	S. KOREA	YES
G-213	SPRUCE	NO	SOSTENUTO	POLYESTER	2	S. KOREA	YES
G-275	SPRUCE	NO	SOSTENUTO	POLYESTER	2	S. KOREA	YES

ADDITIONAL FEATURES: 1-REINFORCED KEY FRAME PIN, 2-STRIKE POINT ADJUSTER, 3-THE G-185 HAS A SOFT CLOSE FALLBOARD.

OTHER ITEMS TO ORDER

Polish $14.95
For newer high-gloss finishes with "anti-static" quality to repel dust.
Polish is excellent for digital piano cases, guitars, drums, etc.

Grand Piano Dust Cover $29.95
 Fits up to seven-foot grands. Protects harp, strings, tuning pins, and soundboard while piano is in use. Easy to clean. Specify color: black, brown, white, red, burgundy.

Order additional books: $ 9.95

  *Prices subject to change. Price does not include shipping.

Order from: SUNSET PUBLISHING
              P.O. Box 1505
              Salt Lake City, Utah 84110